The Bible Speaks Today

Series Editors: J. A. Motyer (OT)
John R. W. Stott (NT)

The Message of Colossians and Philemon

Fullness and Freedom

Kevin Ray

Titles in this series

The Message of Colossians and Philemon

Fullness and Freedom

R. C. Lucas

Rector of St Helen's Church, Bishopsgate, London

Inter-Varsity Press
Leicester, England
Downers Grove, Illinois, U.S.A.

Inter-Varsity Press
38 De Montfort Street, Leicester LE1 7GP, England
Box 1400, Downers Grove, Illinois 60515, U.S.A.

Inter-Varsity Press, England, is the publishing division of the Universities and Colleges Christian Fellowship (formerly the Inter-Varsity Fellowship), a student movement linking Christian Unions in universities and colleges throughout the United Kingdom and the Republic of Ireland, and a member movement of the International Fellowship of Evangelical Students. For information about local and national activities write to UCCF, 38 De Montfort Street, Leicester LE1 7GP.

InterVarsity Press, U.S.A., is the book-publishing division of Inter-Varsity Christian Fellowship, a student movement active on campus at hundreds of universities, colleges and schools of nursing. For information about local and regional activities, write IVCF, 233 Langdon St., Madison, WI 53703.

Distributed in Canada through InterVarsity Press, 860 Denison St., Unit 3, Markham, Ontario L3R 4H1, Canada.

Text set in Great Britain

Printed and bound in Great Britain
by Billing & Sons Limited, Worcester.

UK ISBN 0-85110-736-2 (paperback)
USA ISBN 0-87784-284-1 (paperback)
USA ISBN 0-87784-925-0 (set of The Bible Speaks Today, paperback)

24 23 22 21 20 19 18 17 16 15 14 13 12 11 10 9
15 14 13 12 11 10 09 08 07 06 05 04 03 02

*For Evelyn,
in memory
of Gerald*

General preface

The Bible Speaks Today describes a series of both Old Testament and New Testament expositions, which are characterized by a threefold ideal: to expound the biblical text with accuracy, to relate it to contemporary life, and to be readable.

These books are, therefore, not 'commentaries', for the commentary seeks rather to elucidate the text than to apply it, and tends to be a work rather of reference than of literature. Nor, on the other hand, do they contain the kind of 'sermons' which attempt to be contemporary and readable, without taking Scripture seriously enough.

The contributors to this series are all united in their convictions that God still speaks through what he has spoken, and that nothing is more necessary for the life, health and growth of Christians than that they should hear what the Spirit is saying to them through his ancient—yet ever modern—Word.

J. A. MOTYER
J. R. W. STOTT
Series Editors

Contents

Author's preface

FIRST, a question. Do we need yet more expositions and elucidations of the New Testament letters? If I asked myself this before taking on the responsibility of writing this book I ask it no more.

For one thing the new surge of spiritual life thankfully evident all around us, and not only among young people, demands that we pay particular heed to Paul's letters. Were not most of them written precisely to meet the problems as well as to develop the possibilities of very young churches? This, I think, is why these letters will come into their own in a special way as the tide turns. And we shall need to get out of the habit of reading them verse by verse picking and choosing material to support already accepted positions. They must be allowed to speak for themselves, as they did in the beginning, urgent letters with coherent themes to Christian believers very like ourselves. In this sense how badly the Bible needs to be set free to speak its message today! Then we might hope for a reformation greater if possible than that of the sixteenth century, and an evangelical awakening even more far reaching than that of the eighteenth century.

For another thing, is there not an alarming ignorance of the Scriptures in our modern world, something that shows itself among young converts to Christ? Biblical illiteracy must be almost the church's greatest danger. If this exposition kindles in any Christian reader an enthusiasm to search the Scriptures yet more determinedly in order to 'see if these things be so', I shall be most thankful.

Secondly, an apology. When I first set out to prepare this book I was earnestly charged by a member of the same reading party not to produce 'stodge'—a protest, I suppose, at certain theological works that this friend had failed to enjoy or digest. At the time I found no difficulty in promising to be attractive and readable. How ashamed I now feel! But if the first job of the commentator is to elucidate what the apostle was saying to the people of his own day, then I can report that I have done my best to do this, even if it has meant jettisoning much of the material a preacher might use to illustrate and apply his themes. My reward will depend upon whether or not it becomes clear how pertinently Paul speaks to our own day.

Finally, some sincere acknowledgments. First and foremost to John Stott, to whom I am indebted for the invitation to contribute to this excellent series, as well as for patience and constant encouragement all the way to the finish. It is an enviable privilege for any author to have such skilful advice and friendly counsel available. Further, I owe more than I know to all who have written on this epistle, many of whose works are not quoted here in the footnotes. In addition to the books listed in the Chief Abbreviations I have valued among others the expositions of Alford, Carson, Ellicott, Hendriksen, A. M. Hunter, Knight, Maclaren, R. P. Martin, Bishop Handley Moule, Radford, and Lukyn Williams. No doubt many an idea imagined as one's own was first suggested by a phrase or note in a long-forgotten commentary.

My friend Malcolm Harrison first drew my attention to the recent commentary by Lohse that joins Lightfoot as one of the two books to which I have returned most often for help. He also advised me over articles in scholarly journals that I would not normally see; I am grateful to him for his enthusiastic help.

The dedication recalls the fact that it was in the Schluter family home in Nairobi that most of this book was finally written, with only the colourful birds of East Africa to distract my attention. The generosity and stimulus received from these longstanding friends was chiefly responsible for the pleasure I had in writing this book—and for the endurance I needed.

Frances Shaw gave timely and willing help in typing my first draft, for which I remain grateful, and Janet Prime has so cheerfully and expertly continued to type copy after copy, that I must express particular thanks to her for this special effort amongst all the help she gives the staff and myself here at St Helen's.

Though the phrase may be hackneyed, it is necessary to say that the conclusions I have come to remain entirely my own responsibility.

R.C.L.

Chief abbreviations

Abbott   *A Critical and Exegetical Commentary on the Epistles to the Ephesians and to the Colossians* by T. K. Abbott (*The International Critical Commentary*, T. & T. Clark, 1897).

AV   The Authorized (King James') Version of the Bible, 1611.

Beare   *The Epistle to the Colossians, Introduction and Exegesis* by Francis W. Beare (*Interpreter's Bible*, Abingdon Press, New York and Nashville, 1955).

Bruce   *Commentary on the Epistles to the Ephesians and the Colossians* by E. K. Simpson and F. F. Bruce (Marshall, Morgan & Scott, 1957).

Calvin   *Commentaries on the Epistles to the Philippians, Colossians and Thessalonians* by John Calvin, 1548, translated by John Pringle, 1851 (Eerdmans, 1957).

GNB   The Good News Bible (Today's English Version), (NT 1966, 4th edition 1976; OT 1976: The Bible Societies and Collins).

JBP   *The New Testament in Modern English* by J. B. Phillips (Collins, 1958).

LB   The Living Bible, paraphrased by K. N. Taylor (Coverdale House Publishers, revised British edition 1974).

Lightfoot   *Saint Paul's Epistles to the Colossians and to Philemon* by J. B. Lightfoot, 1879 edition (Zondervan).

Lohse	*Colossians and Philemon, A Commentary* by E. Lohse (*Hermeneia*, Fortress Press, 1971).
Moule	*The Epistles of Paul the Apostle to the Colossians and to Philemon* by C. F. D. Moule (Cambridge University Press, 1957).
NBD	*The New Bible Dictionary* ed. by J. D. Douglas (Inter-Varsity Press, 1962).
NEB	The New English Bible (NT 1961, 2nd edition 1970; OT 1970).
Neill	*Paul to the Colossians* by Stephen Neill (World Christian Books, Lutterworth, 1963).
RSV	The Revised Standard Version of the Bible (NT 1946, 2nd edition 1971; OT 1952).
RV	The Revised Version of the Bible (NT 1881; OT 1885).
Scott	*To the Colossians, to Philemon and to the Ephesians* by E. F. Scott (*Moffat New Testament Commentary*, Hodder and Stoughton, 1952).

The letter to the Colossians

Colossians 1:1–2
But why did he write?

PAUL, an apostle of Christ Jesus by the will of God, and Timothy our brother, ²To the saints and faithful brethren in Christ at Colossae: Grace to you and peace from God our Father.

A customary greeting introduces us to one of Paul's most powerful and attractive letters, written from prison to a young church in the province of Asia. This Christian community in Colossae had come into existence during that period of prodigious missionary and evangelistic activity associated with the apostle's Ephesian ministry (c. AD 52 to 55). So effective were the daily evangelistic 'dialogues' held in the hall of Tyrannus, where Paul's bold speaking compelled men's attention during the long siesta period (the first lunch-hour lectures recorded), that it is possible for Luke to claim that 'all the residents of Asia heard the word of the Lord, both Jews and Greeks' (Acts 19:8–10). Since Paul was notable for sharing his ministry, converts were soon trained and equipped to be his associates in spreading the gospel far and wide.

Possibly it was early in this period that a man named Epaphras, who had come from Colossae in the Lycus valley, was brought to faith in Christ. A hard worker (4:13, a fact which doubtless appealed to the writer of 1 Corinthians 15:10), he seems quickly to have developed into a mature servant of Christ (4:12), and to have been acknowledged by Paul as one of his valued fellow servants (1:7). It was this man whose privilege it was to become the evangelist to his own people.

The immediate result of the ministry of Epaphras was the planting of new churches in Laodicea and Hierapolis as well as at Colossae. For these congregations Epaphras worked and prayed with good success: we know this because some years later (*c.* AD 62), on a visit to Paul who was now under house arrest in Rome,[1] he can report on that hallmark of genuine Christian life, *love*, as being characteristic of these believing communities (1:8).

But there were other, more disturbing, tendencies which Epaphras would describe as he asked counsel of the great apostle. And because it was his own deep concern over these reports that led Paul to write his letter to Colossae, we who now study it need, as far as is possible, to understand what these tendencies were.

The nature of the 'Colossian heresy' has been discussed for over a hundred years since Lightfoot wrote his great commentary on Colossians (1875). But it is still not known exactly what was the 'false teaching' that threatened the peace and stability of the Colossian Christians and their near neighbours. Recently, in an intriguing paper,[2] Dr M. D. Hooker of Cambridge has challenged the almost universally held opinion that the faith of the Christians at Colossae was under such attack from false teachers. Adopting a more cautious approach, she argues that there were no such heretics in the Colossian community. She points out that, unlike the situation with the Galatians, there is no evidence that the church at Colossae had succumbed to distressing error. Evidence is also lacking for the existence of false teaching with regard to Christ. Dr Hooker concludes that a more likely explanation is that young converts were under external pressure to conform 'to the beliefs and practices of their pagan and Jewish neighbours'. Paul's emphasis on the uniqueness and supremacy of Christ's work in creation and redemption is therefore to be seen as a reminder that they had no need to look elsewhere for completion of salvation outside of Christ.

There is much that is appealing in this thesis. Certainly there is nothing in Colossians of the strong indignation found in Paul's letter to the Galatians where he sees the very foundations of orthodox faith being shaken. The Colossian letter is rightly called a 'friendly' letter. Paul's plea for continued loyalty is made to those who can be called, for the most part, *faithful brethren.*

[1] The place of Paul's imprisonment when he wrote this Colossian letter has been much debated: but the traditional view, that Paul writes from Rome, still seems open to fewest objections.

[2] M. D. Hooker, 'Were there false teachers in Colossae?' *Christ and Spirit in the New Testament. Studies in honour of C. F. D. Moule*, ed. B. Lindars and S. S. Smalley (CUP, 1973), pp. 315f.

Yet I doubt if the position can be sustained that there was no real threat from harmful teaching at Colossae. The evidence seems too strong that the young Christians were in danger of being imposed upon by brilliant but delusive preaching (2:4): a new 'philosophy' was being expounded that owed more to religious traditionalism than to Christ (2:8).

Perhaps the real mistake was ever to think of the 'Colossian heresy' in too pagan terms. The curious amalgam of error, superstition and heathen mythology which some commentators have suggested as the threat to the Colossian Christians would not deceive the youngest convert, far less a church grounded in Christian truth by the conscientious Epaphras. We must give these early believers some credit for being able to recognize religious twaddle when they heard it, especially when they had been so recently delivered from it.

Is it that those who write commentaries so seldom pastor churches? The danger to 'faithful brethren', rooted and grounded in Christ, lies not so much in false teaching from *outside* the boundaries of the Christian church; Jehovah's Witnesses, for example, with their failure to confess Christ as more than the highest created being, make their converts among lapsed churchgoers and dissatisfied pagans, seldom from true believers. No, the danger for the enthusiastic young convert comes from error *within* the churches, teaching that is largely, even emphatically, Christian, but *which has been influenced more than it knows by the spirit of the age.*

This, I believe, was the situation in the Lycus valley. It was not that these Christians were so fickle and volatile that they were tempted so soon to give a fresh hearing to Jewish or pagan teachers: it was that the whole syncretistic religious environment in which their churches existed threatened the purity of the new faith.

Surely this must always be the case. The churches of Christ can never be immune from the intellectual and spiritual pressures and fashions of their time. While we see this clearly when we look back to earlier generations, it is less easy for us to recognize this frankly in our own times.

Now this threat would become a genuine peril, and a cause of division, only when leaders began to arise *from within the Christian communities*, teaching with zeal and conviction a spirituality that owed rather more to the spirit of the age (and

21

behind this, as Christians know, to hostile evil powers) than to the teaching of Christ (2 : 8). It was because of the prevailing climate of thought that this new and vigorous presentation of the faith 'rang so many bells' and 'made such sense', and therefore found a ready hearing.

As an illustration, we may take the evidence, noticed by many commentators, of an incipient Gnosticism[3] at Colossae (the fully developed system did not pose its greatest threat to the church until the second and third centuries). Dr Norman Perrin has it exactly right when he says, 'In its early stages Gnosticism was not so much a movement as a mood.'[4] It was this mood, so widely influential, that was drawing certain Christian teachers, not to a greater spirituality as they imagined, but actually away from Christ. Of course they did not see things in this way. But Paul, with God-given wisdom, recognized the peril. So he writes this now famous letter with its affectionate warnings, its clear teaching, its pointed diagnoses, and above all its sustained appeal for loyalty to the truth that had first won the Colossians' allegiance.

The evidence, both for the errors that were making so great an appeal, and for the particular thought-forms of the day that were so easily left unquestioned, must be found *within* the Colossian epistle. We can discern them only as we study the way in which Paul makes his response to them. There are obvious difficulties in this. 'Reading between the lines' is a habit that calls for some caution! Dogmatism will normally be unwise. Yet the attempt has to be made. The careful student of Colossians will need to compile for himself a list of those leading features of the new 'spirituality' that was being so strongly commended. By way of introduction, with no suggestion of finality, here are some of the more easily recognizable threads that run through the whole letter.

First, the new teachers[5] offered a spiritual *'fullness'* not previously experienced. 'Fullness of life' (2 : 10) may well have

[3]See the article on Gnosticism in *NBD*. Gnosticism was an early Christian heresy, whereby certain people claimed private enlightenment of deeper, even secret, truths not known to the ordinary believer, which could be discovered by submission to an initiation at their hands.

[4]Norman Perrin, *The New Testament, an Introduction* (Harcourt, Brace, Jovanovich, Inc., 1974), p. 124.

[5]Normally I prefer 'new teachers' (sometimes 'visitors') as being a less misleading description than 'false teachers'. The new teachers may have been members of one of the local congregations or from further afield. What is certain is that the new teaching had only recently arisen or arrived on the scene.

been one of their slogans. This emphasis on 'fullness' is so pervasive in the letter, and obviously so important if we are to assess the significance of the new 'spirituality', that a longer quotation from the inimitable Bishop Stephen Neill may be in order.

> One thing is quite clear. The false teachers came in with the claim that they would complete and perfect the simple and elementary faith to which the Colossians had been introduced by Paul and his friends. This is what the false teachers always do. 'What you have is quite all right, and a good foundation for faith. Now let us just finish it off for you, and you really will be Christians.' We have seen how this happened among the Galatians. (See *Paul to the Galatians*, W.C.B. No. 25.) In our tragically divided state today, exactly the same thing can happen in the younger churches, though being rather politer than the apostle we shall probably talk of 'Christians of other communions' rather than of false teachers. In many areas where Protestant missions have been at work, Roman Catholic missionaries have later come in, and set themselves to 'complete' the imperfect Christianity of the Protestant converts. Where older Churches have been at work, Christians of the Pentecostal groups have come in, and assured the converts that, unless they speak with tongues, they can have no assurance that they have received the Holy Spirit. Anglicans have been known to convey the blessings of episcopacy to those who thought that they were getting on very nicely without them. All this is very sad; but it may help us to realize that we are not really so very far from the New Testament and its problems.[6]

Secondly, the visitors spoke of a new spiritual *'freedom'* which those who followed them would enjoy. They may have offered 'deliverance' of some kind, since Paul repeatedly reminds the Colossians of the deliverance that is already theirs in Christ (*e.g.* 1:13; 2:15). The apostle is at his most startling when he accuses these preachers of 'liberty' of actually trying to capture believers for what would turn out to be a new 'slavery' (2:8, 18, 20ff.)

[6]Neill, p. 11.

Thirdly, the visitors appear to have claimed particular insight into the powers of evil, and to be able to give believers special protection from them. It is noticeable how Paul designates Christ as the only one with full authority over such powers (*e.g.* 2:10, 15), a triumph in which *all* who are 'in Christ' share. The letter to the Colossians leaves little room for privileges that belong only to a spiritual élite.

Fourthly, the visitors were known for their impressive asceticism: fasting, for instance, seems to have been highly commended if not commanded (as against Paul for whom fasting was, in the only references we have, largely involuntary). At the same time, like all 'perfectionist' theories ever since, this teaching had a poor record in combating self-indulgence, not least in terms of religious vanity (2:18, 23; *cf.* 3:5-8).

The visitors also offered a further initiation into a deeper 'knowledge' of God, and a greater experience of his power. Paul is at his most effective in countering such claims (2:8-15), and in distinguishing between what is already ours in Christ, and what we must yet seek (1:9-14).

Further, the visitors were inclined to be superior to, even critical of, 'ordinary' believers. But their offers of spectacular advance were, to Paul, merely steps *back* into the shadows (2:16-17). Here, as in other letters (*e.g.* 2 Corinthians) the apostle is concerned lest the 'hope' and confidence of those 'in Christ' should be denied either by 'superlative apostles' or by Christians claiming a more complete initiation into the secrets of God.

Finally, the visitors were, unhappily, *divisive* in their influence. Disruption in the fellowship must be part of the cost of listening to them. It would be no exaggeration to say that the whole Colossian letter is a plea for Christian unity (*e.g.* 2:1-5; 3:9-17).

The reader may become weary of these themes by the time this book is finished. But if it seems that I labour them by constant repetition, I can only say that the text of the epistle has forced this upon me. Several times I have found myself saying, 'Not again, Paul!' as the apostle returns to familiar ground and leaves his readers no chance of evading or forgetting his meaning. It is as though he thinks the theme of Christ's sufficiency to be of such importance that its implications must be spelt out at every opportunity. We shall be unwise to be impatient with this steady apostolic persistence.

These seven 'identification marks' may help the reader to recognize some of the issues at stake as he reads what is a particularly concentrated and densely written letter. They are given to alert the student to the extraordinary power of this letter to speak to the contemporary church. If, as orthodox Christians are committed to believing, this ancient epistle to the saints at Colossae is God's word to the churches today, we need not be surprised if it turns out to be, not a museum specimen witnessing to past events and to another world, but a pertinent message for ourselves today.

For me it has been the road back to a new loyalty to evangelical Christianity. In the course of my life I have been influenced in various directions away from my evangelical foundations by Christian men of great spiritual devotion and zeal. By contrast, my commitment to New Testament faith has been immeasurably deepened by the study and teaching of this letter over the last four years. Again and again I have been amazed by the uncanny way in which Paul's teaching and warnings might have been freshly minted for our guidance today, often in areas where Christian people of equal sincerity have found themselves, to their puzzlement and dismay, in different minds. And since, among all Christian people, loyalty to Christ is the chief thing, I have some hopes that through this new study of the Colossian letter, all believing people of good will may find the Bible speaking to them today.

Colossians 1:3-8
True Christians and the true gospel

WE always thank God, the Father of our Lord Jesus Christ, when we pray for you, 4because we have heard of your faith in Christ Jesus and of the love which you have for all the saints, 5because of the hope laid up for you in heaven. Of this you have heard before in the word of the truth, the gospel 6which has come to you, as indeed in the whole world it is bearing fruit and growing—so among yourselves, from the day you heard and understood the grace of God in truth, 7as you learned it from Epaphras our beloved fellow servant. He is a faithful minister of Christ on our behalf 8and has made known to us your love in the Spirit.

Paul follows the custom of his day by beginning his letter to the Christians at Colossae with words of thankfulness for the good news he has had of them. Not that there is anything formal or insincere about these introductory words, for thankfulness was always a special characteristic of Paul's, as well as something he expected from other believers (there is a considerable emphasis on this Christian quality later on in the letter). In any case, the apostle had just heard good news of the Colossians from their mutual friend Epaphras, and, in consequence, is full of gratitude to God for the report of vigorous spiritual life among them.

If this expression of thankfulness comes from the heart, it is also extremely shrewd. There is nothing sterotyped about Paul's thanksgivings; for he likes to make full use of the customary form to serve his own special purposes in writing. Here every word and phrase counts, and it is fascinating to see how it is done.

It appears that high among Paul's aims in writing this letter was that of reassuring the loyal believers at Colossae as to their proper standing as Christians, and to confirm the accuracy of the message brought to them by Epaphras.

Evidently the influence of the new teaching was unsettling on both counts. Its effect had been to raise painful doubts among the young Christians as to whether or not Epaphras had given them the whole truth, that is, a full and complete gospel. Should it turn out that he had failed them in this, the question must inevitably arise as to whether they were equipped with a full and proper experience of the new life in the Spirit.

It is only when studied against this background that the Colossian thanksgiving comes alive. It is an impressive piece of re-assurance. In it Paul explains the reasons why, from reports received, he has no cause to doubt both that they are true Christians, and that what they had heard from the lips of Epaphras was indeed the authentic apostolic message.

1. Paul reassures the Colossians that they are true Christians (verses 3-5a)

We have heard, he writes, *of your faith in Christ Jesus and of the love which you have for all the saints, because of the hope laid up for you in heaven.* Faith, hope and love, make up a familiar triad in Paul's writings (*e.g.* 1 Cor. 13:13; 1 Thes. 1:3). We might almost call them an example of apostolic 'shorthand'. When Paul combines these three elements of Christian spirituality, as in this context, it is usually to provide a basic, and sufficient, description of the genuine Christian. These three qualities are the hallmarks, and proper evidences, of a work of God in the soul of man. More than this may not be required in assessing the worth of a believer's claim to be a true child of God.

None of these three characteristics is thought of by Paul as being natural to us, or even capable of being developed by us. Of course some by temperament may be 'born to believe', some marked out by a particularly affectionate nature, while others are known for a hopeful or optimistic outlook. But Paul is not thinking in these terms at all. To use his own definitions he is describing here not the 'natural' but the 'spiritual' man.

First, such a person is known by his or her *faith in Christ*. This faith is a certain consequence (rather than a cause) of God's work in a person's life. It is not Paul's teaching here that our faith in

Christ leads to an experience of God's Spirit, true though that may be in another context (*e.g.* Jn. 6:37); his purpose now is to show what he regards as an unchallengeable evidence of the work of the Spirit. What Paul is claiming is that a genuine spiritual work of grace can be recognized by the presence of *faith*. In particular the truly spiritual person is led to put his faith in *Christ*. To say 'I believe in God' is not therefore sufficient evidence of one's Christian standing, unless by 'God' is meant *the Father of our Lord Jesus Christ* (*e.g.* verse 3). Those whose faith is in Christ Jesus acknowledge no other God.

It is pedantic to say that Christ is not the object of faith here because the phrase 'in Christ' normally refers to the sphere in which Christians live (*e.g.* verse 2). True, Paul never ceases to remind the Christians in Colossae that everything God gives to us, and everything we receive from God, is 'in Christ' or 'in him' (a phrase repeatedly used throughout the letter). In that environ-ment, however, the only faith recognized as authentic is faith in *Christ* as its sufficient object.

Faith in Christ then is a sign of true spiritual life. But so also, to Paul's delight, is their *love*. He characterizes this love as that which the young Christians at Colossae show *for all the saints, i.e.* for their fellow Christians. This is something the world cannot know. Naturally most people know the joys of family love, and some may be known for a love which is truly self-sacrificial. But unless they are Christ's they cannot share the love of the Christian brotherhood, that distinctive gift of the Spirit to every child of God. It is this that binds people of different national and cultural backgrounds into a fellowship which is unique (3:11).

These Spirit-given qualities of *faith* and *love* which are now theirs mean that the Colossians have been brought by the power and grace of God into a relationship, not only with Christ in heaven, but also with his people on earth. But these marvellously restored lines of communication are theirs here and now only *because of the hope laid up for* them *in heaven* (verse 5a), that is, something hidden in the future, and as yet out of reach.

It is of real importance for present-day Christians to be reminded that a genuine spiritual experience is marked by 'hope' as much as by 'faith' and 'love'. This is seldom the emphasis in modern Christian teaching, as we see from the numerous sermons, studies, and books, on 'faith' and 'love', compared with the few on Christian 'hope'. 'Hope' in Paul's vocabulary has to do with the ultimate future; it is that confident assurance and expectancy of the vaster blessings in store for believers in the life of the world to come (*cf.* Rom. 8:24-25 where it is our present experience of salvation that gives us this keen anticipation of a more complete redemption in the future life).

What is unexpected here is that Paul's language forbids us to think of our hope as a consequence of faith and love, but rather the reverse. The Christian's present taste of reality in fellowship with God and his people is but an anticipation of the substantial realities which are reserved for the future, 'laid up' in heaven for us. Therefore, we are not to think of ourselves as largely enjoying the fruits of Christ's victory now, with heaven as some glorious consummation, a kind of finishing touch. Rather we are to recognize that heaven holds most of the great things won for us by Christ, and that our present experience is no more than a precious foretaste of what is to come.

To grasp this is to gain a very different perspective from that of today, when this world easily means all. And throughout this letter, with its strong emphasis on hope (*e.g.* 1:27), Paul is evidently concerned that his Colossian friends should balance their faith and love with hope. Presumably therefore Paul reckoned the danger of a false perspective to be a real one. With a proper understanding of the balance between 'experience' and 'expectancy', the Colossians will be able to estimate more sensibly the new enthusiasms around them. If the new teaching claimed to offer a fullness of experience in this world that in reality belongs only to the next the Colossians will have needed this protection from disillusionment. Perhaps the visitors scoffed at the notions of 'patient waiting' which the Colossians had learned, and urged upon them the right to 'claim now' a completeness of Christian experience.

But for Paul, as for the other New Testament writers, just because the gospel treasures are to be found in Christ at God's right hand, and will be visibly manifested only at his coming (3:4), the present life of the Christian is *a life of faith*. And faith, by definition, means that the object of our faith is not yet in our possession (Heb. 11:1).

Similarly the Christian learns not to look within himself for evidence of divine *love*. The love that is a genuine evidence of divine working focuses on the brotherhood. It is not so much a mystical experience of God whom we have not seen as the practical actions of love toward our brothers and sisters whom we can see.

In this first description of what is genuine Christian experience Paul puts Christ, the Christian brotherhood, and heaven, as the objects respectively of faith, love, and hope, thus discouraging his Colossian friends from concentrating upon subjective experience in a search for Christian fullness of life. If the risen Christ, their Christian brethren, heaven, are the centre of their spiritual concerns then they may know that they possess an authentic spirituality in accordance with Paul's gospel.

2. Paul reassures the Colossians that they have heard the true gospel (verses 5b-8)

It seems likely that the visitors had cast doubts on the completeness of the Christian message as delivered to the Colossians by Epaphras. Since the young church had never yet seen or heard the great apostle in person, it would be easy for these new and enthusiastic critics to drive a wedge between Paul and his fellow servant. The impression could be given that there was considerably more in Paul's gospel than Epaphras had yet reported. So the Colossians would be bewildered, wondering whether or not what they had heard was an adequate account of the apostolic message.

Against this background Paul's carefully chosen words gain new significance. *Of this (hope) you have heard before in the word of the truth, the gospel which has come to you, as indeed in the whole world*, he writes (verses 5b-6a). Notice first that this gospel had come to them as a *word*, that is, by preaching and teaching which called for a listening and understanding response. God's power had been brought close to them by a proclamation, not by an act or deed. Rather, God's word was his deed (*cf.* the important Rom. 1 : 16).

This proclamation concerned *the truth*, absolute and final. Could simpler words make a grander claim? The gospel of Christ is nothing less than the truth, beyond human invention and imagination. In this context it is useful to recall the familiar phrase, 'the truth, the whole truth, and nothing but the truth.' The gospel is just this, so we can neither add to it, nor subtract from it, without doing serious harm to the integrity of that unique proclamation.

This bold claim to possess and preach the *truth* must always be a scandal to men and women in any age, not least our own. But we have to insist that the merits of the gospel cannot be compared with other forms of religious teaching, for while they are relative ('that is truth for you but not for me') Christianity is absolute and therefore universal ('this is truth for all').

It is important to perceive how Paul equates the 'word of the truth' with 'the gospel'. It is sometimes said that we should preach 'good news' (*i.e.* gospel) rather than doctrine. But such a distinction is foreign to Paul. The good news he received and preached was essentially doctrinal in that it consisted of a body of truth (*cf.* the important 1 Cor. 15:1-4). Of course that does not mean that Christian teaching is doctrinaire (*i.e.* theoretical and unpractical). But to divorce the gospel from its historic roots is perilous.

We may then find ourselves proclaiming a living Jesus who enters into lives now to meet present needs, without teaching of the dying Jesus who entered the world once to bear our sins. Nor can there be commitment to the living Christ without commitment to the facts of the third day (1 Cor. 15:17). Jesus asked of his friends, 'Do you believe this?' as well as, 'Do you believe in me?' (Jn. 11:25-27).

This leads on to the next point in Paul's reassurance where he is able to tell the Colossians that the gospel they had heard was the very same gospel that all the other churches in the *whole world* were hearing and receiving. The force of this is greater than might, at first, appear. The Christian gospel has, from the start, been a 'catholic' faith, that is to say, universal in its appeal and scope, whereas it is of the essence of all esoteric versions of the truth that they possess only local and temporary appeal. Variations of the historic faith claiming to offer a more complete gospel prove attractive to certain temperaments and types, they rise and fall at certain times, yet never show themselves to possess a universal validity.

But there is still more food for thought in this remarkable description of apostolic truth and its hallmarks. The authentic gospel has at all times been known by the fact that it is living, and therefore is recognizable by its ability to be constantly *bearing fruit and growing:* and this it had already done in Colossae as well as further afield. 'The fruit, which the gospel bears without fail in all soils and under every climate, is its credential, its verification, as against the pretensions of spurious counterfeits.'[1] The gospel is the true seed, and normally a rich harvest is inevitable when the seed is sown, although there are, of course, fields particularly resistant to this sowing, such as Muslim lands in North Africa. For example, from a recent survey published by the National Christian Council of Kenya in 1973:

> Wherever the Word of God—the preaching of the Good News—went amongst the animistic tribal populations of Kenya, the response was instantaneous, immediate, and enormous.

Again,

> Statistical analysis shows very clearly that although the first seed was originally a foreign import, the resultant Christianity in Kenya cannot be thought of as a foreign transplant, but rather must be seen as an indigenous plant from the very first. Its expansion has not been due primarily to external forces (foreign missions, colonial pressures, western education or civilisation); it has been due primarily to internal forces within the African churches themselves.

And again,

> The startling growth of the churches in Kenya—and across the whole of Black Africa also—is a sign of the arrival of the Kingdom of God in Africa in genuinely indigenous form. It is clear evidence that Christianity has been accepted by Africans from the earliest days as a genuinely African religion, with roots firmly in African soil. This is also striking refutation of the complaints still heard today that Christianity in Kenya is foreign, western, the white man's religion—for, the statistical evidence clearly points to the fact that, literally from the very first days, the seed had successfully taken root in African soil.[2]

This 'spontaneous expansion' of the church is due then to the productive power of the simple gospel message (*cf.* Rom. 1:16).

[1] Lightfoot, p. 135.
[2] *Kenya Churches Handbook* (Evangel Publishing House, Kenya, 1973), pp. 166f.

Presumably, therefore, the implications of Paul's words are that there is no need for the kind of 'enrichment' that the false teachers were claiming to bring.

Such growth the Colossians had experienced among themselves *from the* very first *day they heard and understood the grace of God in truth* (verse 6). The description here is quite emphatic, *understood* being a strong word implying that their grasp of the truth was a firm one; they had a full appreciation, or 'advanced knowledge' of it, so that this was no ordinary, or superficial, level of understanding.

What then was it that the Colossians had so completely taken to heart? In a word, it was *the grace of God in truth*. No single word more accurately defines the essence of the Christian gospel than *grace*. The young church at Colossae had understood 'grace' in its true meaning and simplicity, without any of the false additions that so easily make grace no longer grace. This meant that, from the very beginning, they understood that man can make no claim on God, however sincere or faithful he may think himself to be; that the heart of the gospel concerns not our commitment to God but his free and merciful offer to commit himself to us in Christ; that our acceptance of the Saviour is meaningless unless God has already freely accepted us in him; that the very essence of the story is not that of men striving to make Christ their Lord, but of Christ in sheer goodness and pity, undertaking for his own sake to make us his servants, despite the fact that we never cease to be unprofitable and undeserving of such a privilege.

It was this gospel of the true grace of God that the Colossians had *learned* (notice the word) from the lips of Epaphras. The implication seems to be that this *fellow servant* of Paul's had been a conscientious and thorough teacher of the gospel message. His mission had been no hit-and-run affair with minimal instruction. The truth had been fully explained and applied, and Paul, characteristically, gives due praise to his friend and envoy. Incidentally, this is further evidence that Paul had a great capacity for drawing others to share his concerns, and making them feel partners in the work, and the apostle was exemplary in supporting his junior partners when occasion demanded, as now in Colossae following the likely depreciation of Epaphras by the new teachers.

So this fine missionary and church planter receives from Paul a commendation as a faithful and reliable servant of Christ, one who had acted and spoken as his representative to the apostle's entire satisfaction. Paul can say that he has no fear that Epaphras had failed him; therefore the Colossians need have no fear that Epaphras had failed them either.

The final touch in verse 8 is delightful. Epaphras had carried messages in both directions. Reporting on the state of the Colossians to Paul, he made special reference to their *love in the Spirit*. There could be no surer sign of their living faith and expectant hope than this (*cf.* 1 Cor. 13 : 1-3). So it is as if Paul is asking why, since Epaphras has proved such a reliable reporter about the Colossian church *to him*, he should not be equally trustworthy in reporting the apostolic teaching *to them*.

The significance of Paul's commendation of Epaphras is forcibly captured by Calvin in his exposition of the little phrase 'in truth' (verse 6).

> *In truth* means *truly* and *without pretence*; for as he had previously declared that the gospel is undoubted truth, so he now adds, that it had been purely administered by them, and that *by Epaphras*. For while all boast that they preach the gospel, and yet at the same time there are many *evil workers* (Phil. iii. 2), through whose ignorance, or ambition, or avarice, its purity is adulterated, it is of great importance that faithful ministers should be distinguished from the less upright. For it is not enough to hold the term gospel, unless we know that this is the true gospel—what was preached by Paul and Epaphras. Hence Paul confirms the doctrine of Epaphras by giving it his approbation, that he may induce the Colossians to adhere to it, and may, by the same means, call them back from those profligates who endeavoured to introduce strange doctrines. He at the same time dignifies Epaphras with a special distinction, that he may have more authority among them; and lastly, he presents him to the Colossians in an amiable aspect, by saying that he had borne testimony to him of their love. Paul everywhere makes it his particular aim, that he may, by his recommendation, render those who he knows serve Christ faithfully, very dear to the Churches; as, on the other hand, the ministers of Satan are wholly intent on alienating, by unfavourable representations ('By false reports and calumnies') the minds of the simple from faithful pastors.[3]

[3]Calvin, p. 141.

Colossians 1:9-14
Be filled for this

AND so, from the day we heard of it, we have not ceased to pray for you, asking that you may be filled with the knowledge of his will in all spiritual wisdom and understanding, [10]to lead a life worthy of the Lord, fully pleasing to him, bearing fruit in every good work and increasing in the knowledge of God. [11]May you be strengthened with all power, according to his glorious might, for all endurance and patience with joy, [12]giving thanks to the Father, who has qualified us to share in the inheritance of the saints in light. [13]He has delivered us from the dominion of darkness and transferred us to the kingdom of his beloved Son, [14]in whom we have redemption, the forgiveness of sins.

In his life and letters Paul stands revealed as a great intercessor. What he urged upon others (4:2), he did not fail to practise himself. Nor was he afraid of *asking* in prayer (verse 9), making it his business to be definite in his requests for others. So it is no surprise that, from the moment good news of solid progress had come from Colossae, the apostle began to pray ceaselessly for the young Christians there.

Paul's prayer is as apt and as carefully shaped as his thanksgiving. With the vigilance necessary for effective prayer (4:2) he is aware of the appeal being made by the new missionaries and of its enormous attractiveness. Numerous commentators (*e.g.* Bruce and Beare) have noted that the characteristic offer of the visitors must have been connected with spiritual *fullness*. It appears that their striking claim was to bring much more spiritual treasure to the Colossians than they had been able to enjoy through the elementary ministry of Epaphras. In

35

particular terms, it seems that this offer centred round a deepening of *knowledge* and a manifestation of *power*. When both these additional gifts were operative, so it was claimed, they must inevitably transform the lives of individual Christians, as well as the whole prospect of their little churches in a hostile environment.

Against the background of this new teaching circulating in Colossae, Paul's prayer comes immediately into sharp focus. While he wishes to guard them from delusive offers of 'fullness', he wants nothing less for them than that they should be 'filled' with all the blessings of God in Christ. Paul is no enemy to growth and progress in Christian experience. It is true that he is constantly reminding his readers of what is already theirs in Christ Jesus. But what an absurdity to think of him as an apostle of complacence and self-satisfaction![1] It is important to emphasize this. More than one reader of this book in manuscript form asked if it was correct to believe and teach that a Christian 'has it all' from the moment of his conversion. The truth seems to be that Paul's insistence on the believer's perfect standing in Christ (*e.g.* 1:22; 2:10) will always invite such a reaction as inevitably as his teaching on justification by faith continues to call forth the misunderstandings and protests of Romans 6:1, 15. The balance of Paul's teaching is preserved if the thanksgiving and the prayer are kept in close relationship with one another. It is just because he can thank God for the fullness of what the Colossians have already received in truth and life, that he can pray that the young converts may 'daily increase in the Holy Spirit more and more'. However, the apostle's supreme concern throughout this letter, beautifully summarized in 2:6-7, is that all growth and development of spiritual life should be wholly consistent with its beginnings.

This prayer is best understood as taking up the two themes of 'knowledge' and 'power'. The use of the word *all* is particularly revealing. Paul prays that the Christians *may be filled with the knowledge of God's will in all spiritual wisdom and understanding,* and also that they may be *strengthened with all power.* His intense longing (for it is as strong as this) is that, in these two realms, the young believers should possess and experience nothing less than 'full measure'.

---

[1] *Cf.* Phil. 3:12-16; Eph. 5:18-20.

1. The realm of knowledge

We may surmize that an exciting promise of the visitors was that those willing to accept a further initiation at their hands would come to enjoy a deeper insight or knowledge (*Gk. gnōsis*) of the things of God. From such small beginnings was to grow the developed Gnosticism of the second century which was to set the churches so many problems.[2] Such an appeal has perennial fascination, offering as it does a special understanding of spiritual reality, immune from dissent or discussion, shared only by those similarly 'in the secret'. But Paul will have none of it. In Christ, his friends at Colossae had already received *full knowledge* (*Gk. epignōsis*). Bruce quotes Bultmann's definition of *epignōsis* is 'almost a technical term for the decisive knowledge of God which is involved in conversion to the Christian faith'.[3] It is just because, in Christ, the Christians already have access to the privilege of this 'full knowledge' of God, that Paul can pray for them that they may be filled with it. If conversion to Christ had *not* brought with it this decisive understanding, then it would be reasonable to teach the need for some further initiation, and thus to occupy the same sort of ground as the new teachers. Paul does not ask for the Christians a new knowledge, however, but rather the proper use of what is already theirs in Christ, so that they can the better discern the will of God for their lives.

This kind of apostolic teaching always runs the risk of seeming pedestrian. But in Paul's gospel the goal is no mystic awe-inspiring apprehension of divine mysteries reserved for an elite. It is rather an intelligent grasp of what the will of God demands in daily living. As Lohse puts it, 'In the instruction of primitive Christianity, understanding of the will of God is always connected with the command to follow God's will and to do it'.[4] It is in order to understand how the will of God translates into the everyday business of living in a complex world that the Christian needs *all spiritual wisdom and understanding*. Often found together in the Old Testament, these two words are used to describe the qualities David asked for his son Solomon as he took charge over Israel,[5] and that Solomon himself asked for in the light of his vast responsibilities.[6] Faced daily with difficult problems, and often even more difficult people, Solomon must know how to relate the

[2] See the article on 'Gnosticism' in *NBD*.   [3] Bruce, p. 185, note 29.
[4] Lohse ρ. 26.   [5] 1 Ch. 22:12.   [6] 2 Ch. 1:10.

unchanging principles of God's will, revealed in the law, to the present and quickly changing questions of the day. For such work the best wisdom of the world is insufficient.

The necessity of such understanding for the Colossian Christians is evident when we see the standard of living that is expected of them, as described in verse 10. And, in the context of this letter, it is important to realize that these goals are for every single believer. 'Fullness' of knowledge, therefore, cannot possibly be the preserve of a few, since *all* have to *lead a life worthy of the Lord, fully pleasing to him, bearing fruit in every good work.* There is no conceivable way for anyone to reach verse 10 except through verse 9. So *all* the Christians without exception will need *all* God's wisdom without diminution.

How does Paul expect a Christian to lead, or conduct, his life? The three descriptive phrases in verse 10 are characteristic of the apostle at all times, but seem to have a special place in his letters from prison at this particular time. First, Christian living is only that which is *worthy* of so great a Lord and Master. The obedience Christians practise must be sufficient to give the world an adequate picture of their Lord and his purposes for mankind. For example, to walk worthily of Christ is to walk in harmony with other Christians;[7] disunity in the churches is unworthy of him. This particular concern is very marked in the prison epistles, and will become more and more evident in Colossians: this is no surprise, for where a few make claims of a special 'knowledge' hidden from their brethren, a breach of fellowship is almost unavoidable.

Secondly, Christian living is that which is fully *pleasing* to Christ, another familiar Pauline ambition.[8] Just as we speak of 'studying' to please our friends, so we need to 'study' God's pleasure by searching out his likes and dislikes as he has revealed them. In doing this, we shall, incidentally, be set free from an unhealthy dominance of the natural desire to please others who are particularly influential (*cf.* 3:22).

Thirdly, Christian living is that which, *through the knowledge of God, is constantly bearing fruit and increasing in good deeds* (in preference to the RSV rendering). Here, the emphasis is on the essential link between right beliefs and righteous conduct. In the end, false teaching is known by its fruits, or rather lack of them,

---

[7] *Cf.* Eph. 4:1f.; Phil. 1:27.   [8] *E.g.* 2 Cor. 5:8; 1 Thes. 4:1.

for observation does not discover a clear link between claims to possess *gnōsis* and actual *goodness:* whereas an awareness of God's gracious acts towards us should lead to many gracious acts from us towards others. The evidence God looks for is not so much 'spiritual' as 'practical'. The harvest of wisdom is works. Special knowledge (*gnōsis*) leads usually to conceit,[9] whereas the knowledge of God (*epignōsis*) should lead to love for others rather than for ourselves.

How illuminating Paul is when he tackles the empty claims of these foolish enthusiasts! If *fullness* is desired, let it be life lived in a way that 'fully' pleases God, and is 'filled' with good deeds towards others. Such a pathway is by no means easy to discover and follow, but, in Christ, the wisdom can be found to discern it.[10]

2. The realm of power

Paul lags not one whit behind the visitors in wanting for these young converts a full experience of God's power. *May you be strengthened with all power*, he writes, *according to his glorious might*. It would not be easy, in so few words, to concentrate more emphasis on the possibilities of divine power in human lives. The request is for the empowering of ordinary Christians with *all power, i.e.* fullness of power. It is to be according to a sublime measure, namely that power which it is the glory of God to demonstrate; 'glory' here, it should be noted, stands for something *manifested*[11] to people. Are we to see here reference to the claims of the new teaching to give 'fullness' to the Colossian church, especially in the realm of power manifested in their lives? Whether or not this is so, it is salutary to see what a Christian apostle asks of God for Christians. True, it is not for anything less than that the 'glory' should rest upon them through the enjoyment of God's mighty power. But it is *power for all endurance and patience*. Is this an anti climax? It may seem so, yet it is true to the business of living for Christ in the real world. For that world is one where the Christian needs all of God's almighty power steadily to continue and persevere despite the suffering,

[9] NEB *Cf.* the important 1 Cor. 8:1-3.
[10] If the RSV is preferred, then, in the walking of this pathway, ever new knowledge will become ours.
[11] Lightfoot, p. 140. *Cf.* Eph. 1:6, 17ff.; 3:16.

opposition, shocks and disappointments that must at times be his lot, doing this not with despondency or collapsing morale, but *with joy!*

It is through great endurance that the servant of God commends himself.[12] By it he learns to hold his position under attack, and quietly to persist in the paths of righteousness and truth. Through *patience* the Christian learns forbearance and self-restraint, especially with the people who test him; he also finds here the secret of steadiness when divine promises and hopes are deferred. 'It means the deep breath which enables one to wait patiently.'[13]

It is of the utmost importance, if we are to understand New Testament spirituality, to see that such experience of God's power is a *sine qua non* of the normal Christian life. Since *all* need patience and endurance, *all* must know God's manifested strength. By the same token, all who do steadfastly continue with Christ show by that very fact the 'glory' of God's power resting upon them.

The little phrase 'with joy' cannot be disconnected from the earlier part of verse 11, since joy under pressure and through trial is one of the marvels of God's work in his people. Paul never ceases to celebrate it, and the practical James does not contradict him.[14] At the same time, the phrase is a natural bridgehead into the thanksgiving of verses 12-14, so we can recognize an equally clear connection with what follows.

But why more expressions of thanksgiving when the formal section of thanksgiving is over, and Paul is describing his *prayers* for them? A simple answer would be that Paul is never finished with thanksgiving. He overflows with it. For him it is the characteristic hallmark of the Spirit-filled life (2:7). But I think there is more to it than this. There is a sense in which verses 12-14 make very clear what Paul is *not* praying for. There are certain blessings of the gospel which already belong to the Colossians because of their incorporation into Christ. These spiritual possessions are thankfully to be relied upon as theirs. There can be no question of seeking for these splendid gifts since, in Christ, they are already theirs. To look for them elsewhere would be disloyalty to the one who is their Lord.

The two privileges that they possess refer to the work of the

---

[12] 2 Cor. 6:4.   [13] Lohse, p. 31.   [14] 1:24; *cf.* Rom. 5:3; Jas. 1:2.

Father when, through Christ, he made these Colossians members of his kingdom. The Christians could rightly say

> He has qualified us!
> He has delivered us!

This qualification *to share in the inheritance of the saints in light* means that all the conditions have been met which entitle a person to claim his full standing as an enlightened member of God's chosen people. With the forgiveness of sins, he has been allotted his place in the inheritance of the saints.[15] The significance of this will emerge later, as in 2:18, where it becomes evident that the new teachers troubled the peace of the church by, wittingly or unwittingly, 'disqualifying' the believers. Their teaching had the effect, if not the intention, of making the converts from Epaphras's teaching feel that, in some way, their experience of spiritual life was not full value. It almost seemed that they were second-class citizens in God's kingdom: they were given to understand that they had not appropriated the full inheritance, whereas others had already entered into the promised land of blessing. Now Paul thanks God not for their entrance into a *future* inheritance but for their *present* qualification for it. And he will not allow them to be 'disqualified'. The Lord Jesus Christ is now their portion, and there can be no richer inheritance in this world than that.

Verse 12 takes the good news to a point where, to many serious and sensitive people, it seems too good to be true. There are many Christians who, even if they themselves do not believe in purgatory, are sure that they are 'not qualified for heaven'. Even such a stalwart as C. S. Lewis apparently faltered here.[16] Yet because of the gospel of justification by grace alone, through Christ's death alone and by faith alone,[17] the unassailable verdict of the last day, 'Accepted', can be heard and depended upon here and now. So the apostle Paul believed and taught, as we shall find vividly expressed in verse 22 of this first chapter.

In addition to this it will become evident in chapter 2 that at the heart of the visitors' appeal was an offer of 'deliverance'.

---

[15] *Cf.* the important Acts 26:18.
[16] R. L. Green and W. Hooper, *C. S. Lewis* (Collins, 1974), p. 234.
[17] Rom. 3:24; 5:6-11; 3:28.

41

Essentially the benefit they claimed to bring to the church was one of a new liberty from bondage, a new release from sin and Satan's power. Paul answers this by showing in comprehensive terms just what, in Christ, had already been done for the Colossians. God had *delivered them from the dominion of darkness* and *transferred them to the Kingdom of his beloved Son.* This magnificent description of salvation shows the old life as lived under a tyranny where the powers of darkness reign.[18] Without a divine deliverance there was no escape. But, through Christ these powers have been forced to yield their prey, and see their erstwhile captives released to belong to the realm of a greater king.[19]

This great work of deliverance was achieved at the cross (2:15), and every single man and woman in Christ shares in that triumph. In him *we have redemption.* That is, we have been liberated, or released from bondage. We could not otherwise call ourselves Christians, for this redemption is nothing else than *the forgiveness of sins.*

Verse 14 is important for Christians today because it unites what too often we tend to divide. The blessing of forgiveness has sometimes been devalued, as though it were no more than the wiping of the slate clean. But sin is always *a power* that holds people in thrall, so, in Paul's teaching, forgiveness must include the breaking of that power. It is inconceivable that God should forgive the past, and then send us back incapable of living a new life. Pardon without deliverance would be a mockery, and it is never so contemplated in the New Testament. We ought not to speak of 'mere forgiveness' as though this were but an initial blessing of the gospel. The gospel is precisely the offer of freedom because of the forgiveness of our sins.[20] That forgiveness flows from the cross where Christ not only cancelled our debt but also disarmed our enemy (2:14, 15).

> Nothing can surpass or supplement the forgiveness of sins. This is so because the sovereign rule of Christ is present where there is forgiveness of sins; and with forgiveness of sins everything, life and blessings everlasting, has in fact been granted.[21]

---

[18] Lk. 22:53.   [19] Lohse, p. 37; Lightfoot, p. 141.
[20] *E.g.* Acts 13:38, 39.   [21] Lohse, p. 40.

What is now clear once again is that words which might appear conventional are packed full of meaning. Paul is protecting the young church at Colossae. He cannot stand by while the new teachers speak of a new and superior gift of freedom. Have the believers forgotten what their Lord and Saviour has done for them? Can they be dissatisfied with that great work of redemption at the cross? Is Christ not sufficient both to pardon and to deliver them from all their sins? Then let them be filled with knowledge and power for this—a life of increasing goodness and gratitude to the end.

Colossians 1 : 15–20

Christ, supreme Lord and sufficient Saviour

HE is the image of the invisible God, the first-born of all creation; 16for in him all things were created, in heaven and on earth, visible and invisible, whether thrones or dominions or principalities or authorities—all things were created through him and for him. 17He is before all things, and in him all things hold together. 18He is the head of the body, the church; he is the beginning, the first-born from the dead, that in everything he might be pre-eminent. 19For in him all the fullness of God was pleased to dwell, 20and through him to reconcile to himself all things, whether on earth or in heaven, making peace by the blood of his cross.

Introductions are now over. The customary thanksgivings and prayers are done. As we have seen they were not mere formalities, for they are filled with evidences of Paul's acute understanding of the situation in Colossae. However, it is time now to come to the main purpose of the letter.

We might expect the apostle to begin with an appeal to the Colossian church to avoid the approaching dangers, which should be as obvious to them as they are to him. This, for instance, was his method when writing first to the Corinthians (1 Cor. 1 : 10f.) But in this case he does no such thing. It seems almost as if the new teachers and their attractive spiritual wares are forgotten. Instead Paul launches out into a great description of Christ, fit to stand alongside the famous non-Pauline passages of John 1 : 1–14, and Hebrews 1 : 2–4, being particularly close in structure to the latter.

The reason for this approach must be that Paul well knows that the Colossians are not wilfully unfaithful. It is simply that they are young in the faith, with their convictions as yet unformed and immature. Because of this, the speciousness of the visitors' arguments has not been detected. It had not occurred to the Colossians that to welcome this new teaching was to be disloyal to the old. It seemed to them an exciting fresh revelation of truth taking them on from Epaphras' beginnings.

Paul sees in this dangerous innocence a failure to understand what belief in Christ, and loyalty to that belief, involves. It is therefore his wisdom to set before the church, right at the start of the letter, an exposition of the *supremacy* of Christ, or, as we might put it, his lordship. This positive instruction, once its implications have been grasped in terms of the *sufficiency* of Christ, will be the Colossians' best protection against error.

Questions have been raised as to whether this summary statement is Paul's own composition. Was it perhaps already in existence, as teaching material for memorizing, or even as a Christian hymn? (If it was a spiritual song along the lines of 3 : 16 it would make the teaching hymns of even a Charles Wesley appear lightweight.)

If so, then this description of Christ was already well known to the Colossians, and Paul's appeal would be the more forceful, since he would be calling the church back to truths to which they were already willingly committed. However, so exactly do these words suit the needs of the Colossians, and so perfectly do they form a foundation for the rest of this particular letter, that it seems more likely that Paul is either freely adapting traditional material on constructing with God-given wisdom his own explanation of the glory of Christ.

Far more important, as has often been noted,[1] is the fact that within three decades of the crucifixion, language like this was in normal circulation among the churches to describe Jesus of Nazareth. What such testimony shows is that there never was a time, from the beginning of the church's life, when the highest honours of the Godhead were not given to his name.

To come to terms with a confession of faith like this, so concentrated and weighty, it may be useful first to set out the basic framework, even if inadequately, and then to suggest three important clues as to the significance of the statement as a whole.

[1] *E.g.* Moule, p. 48.

1. *Christ supreme*
   a. In creation (verses 15–17)
   b. In the church, the new creation (verse 18)
2. *Christ sufficient*
   a. In his person, God with us (verse 19)
   b. In his work, God for us (verse 20)

1. The first clue: the connection between the supremacy and the sufficiency of Christ

It is often said that the theme of the Colossian epistle is the pre-eminence of Christ. He is supreme in authority over all things, as expressed in verses 15–18. But this confession that Christ is the true Lord of all is the essential foundation of all Christian discipleship.[2] We must assume therefore that, in principle, the church at Colossae was built on this foundation since no other foundation for such wise building exists.[3] If the believers had denied Christ's pre-eminence, then they would hardly be Christian at all. Yet of the reality of their faith we, like them, are already assured (verse 4).

So it would be truer to say that the theme of this letter is the *sufficiency*, or adequacy, of Christ as Saviour. This means that no other spiritual power whatsoever is necessary to bring to mankind God's full and final salvation. What was happening in Colossae was that the Christians seemed ready to deny the sufficiency of Christ for all their spiritual needs, and therefore, in practice, to deny the supremacy of Christ to which they were already committed.

It is for this reason that Paul drives home the lesson that just because Christ is the supreme Lord he must be a sufficient Saviour. He urges the Colossians to remember *who Christ is*. On such a basis he then calls upon them to recognize what such a Christ does for them (with implied astonishment that they should look anywhere other than Christ).

To take one example: if Christ is the supreme Lord of all on whom all other heavenly powers depend, then he cannot require assistance from any of these dependent authorities in order to bring God to people and people to God. He is a sufficient Saviour because he is a supreme Lord.

[2] 1 Cor. 12:3.   [3] 1 Cor. 3:10–11.

To take another example, if Christ's is the power which sustains the whole universe from remote beginnings to its final goal (verse 17), is it reasonable to doubt his power to sustain the individual believer from conversion to glory? Put in this way it would, of course, be absurd, even monstrous, to deny the adequacy of Christ. But, as we shall see, something like that was happening.

The connection between Christ's supremacy and his sufficiency is a vital clue for the student of Colossians. Possessing pre-eminent authority, Christ must be a perfect Saviour. His sufficient adequacy depends on his supreme authority.

2. The second clue: The connection between Christ as Creator and as Redeemer

Separating the various sections of this confessional statement for analysis can be dangerous if it leads us to divide what Paul has joined together. A particularly important connection here, relevant to the whole letter, is that between Christ as Creator and as Redeemer. For if the source of the universe, as well as of the universal church, is to be found 'in him' (verse 16) then we owe to Christ our physical existence and joys, just as much as our spiritual life. Thus both the 'material' and the 'spiritual' realms are brought firmly under the sovereignty of Christ. In view of this, the student of Colossians will look with special care for those tell-tale signs of the 'dualism' in thought and practice which was threatening the young church. It seems certain that among the new teachers were the first of a multitude of guides who, often unwittingly, have troubled the Christian church ever since, by making a false distinction between the two realms, sometimes called 'secular' and 'sacred'. When this happens a whole way of thinking becomes possible that is not Christian. For example, religion becomes too 'spiritual' in a wrong and mischievous sense. Compared with spiritual gifts God's good gifts in the material world are little valued (2 : 21); God's realm is thought of increasingly in churchly terms such as traditional ritual and religious festivals (2 : 16-18); the 'religious' life comes to belong to the specialist in prayer, fasting, and mystical exercises rather than to the normal Christian (described in chapter 3) with his responsibilities in family life and daily labour; and soon it becomes even easier to neglect one's role as a citizen of this world because of one's membership in the church, and to conclude, to take an instance almost at random, that working for one's living is somehow inferior to living 'by faith'.

By so closely linking the truths of verses 15–17 with verse 18 Paul unites what 'religion' so often divides. With this clue in our possession, parts of the Colossian letter that might at first sight baffle us, more easily yield their meaning.

3. The third clue: Christ, before time, on earth, and over all

One unmistakeable aim of this great confessional statement is to tell us *who Christ is* (note the repeated 'he is' verses 15–18). For purposes of analysis and study we can recognize here the Christ who existed 'before all worlds', the Christ of history, and the Lord of the church alive for evermore. But it really seems as though Paul's fixed intention here is to unite what we so easily divide. When he writes of Christ to the Colossians he wants them to know that it is the full Christ, Creator, Redeemer and ascended Lord, of whom he speaks. He wants them to know that *all* (note the tireless repetition of this little word in every verse, almost every phrase) the activity of almighty God in creating the world, and in visiting and redeeming his people, has been done in and through Christ. So that 'in Christ' (note the repeated '*in him*' for similar emphasis) the young believers in Colossae occupy a position of privilege beyond which nothing can be conceived.

This resolute refusal to divide God's work from Christ, or to divide Christ in respect of the various parts of his work, gives us a clue we need to recognize two forms in which 'fullness' teaching may have reached Colossae. It may have been by a claim that God had not finished his work of salvation for the Colossians in giving them Christ, so that he had still more to give them if his work was to be completed. But the false teaching may have been put in another way. The Colossians may have been told that to receive the benefits of Christ's saving work on the cross was one thing, but that to receive and enjoy the benefits of his reigning work at God's right hand was quite another. To be cleansed from sin was a blessed beginning; but to be delivered from sin's power they must now claim and appropriate the victory of the ascended Lord over the principalities and powers. To be fully saved the Colossians were urged to make the full Christ their own.

Against both these forms of erroneous teaching Paul's testimony stands unshaken. He teaches first that what God has done in Christ exhausts all that God has to do for us. He teaches, secondly, that when a person is in Christ, he or she is the beneficiary of all that God has done in Christ (*cf.* 2 : 9, 10).

a. Christ and creation (verses 15–17)

Though some of the details may be elusive, the main thrust of this section is not difficult to grasp—once the reader has recovered his breath! The whole created order, in time and space, owes its existence to Christ. He is its true origin. He sustains it in being. Without him it would have no ultimate meaning. All this, and much besides, is included in these brief overwhelming affirmations. At this point we will consider not what these verses tell us about creation, but what they tell us about Christ. And here we cannot do better than return to the two key words, *supremacy* and *sufficiency*.

(i) *In creation Christ is supreme.* This settles once and for all the status of those numerous heavenly powers and intermediaries that both fascinated and frightened the people of Paul's day (as often in our own). No attempt should be made to distinguish between the various 'authorities' listed in verse 16. All the church needs to know is that such existence and power as they possess is entirely dependent upon Christ our Lord. It follows that there is nothing such 'powers' can do to influence Christ or enrich him (as some Christians have appeared to suppose in their intercessions to departed saints); from this it further follows that there is nothing they can do to influence the destiny or experience of the person who is 'in Christ'.

Exactly how the Colossian church was being troubled along these lines we do not know. But it is evident that the new teachers claimed an unusual familiarity with the 'powers in the heavenlies', and offered their expertise in these realms to the young Christians. We shall meet this later (*e.g.* 2 : 8).

For the loyal Christian it is enough to know that these 'powers' have neither 'treasures' to give to, nor 'terrors' with which to frighten, the one who lives under the sovereignty of Christ.

(ii) *In creation Christ is sufficient.* Read verses 15–17 again and see with what force Paul repeats the little phrase 'all things'. Whatever aspect of creation we care to think about, Christ is the sufficient explanation. And his power is as adequate as his wisdom.

The full significance of this is beyond our present scope. It is important to realize that the reason why Paul affirms this mighty

49

truth to the Colossians is more practical than philosophical. He writes to Christians who can honestly say 'Christ is my helper', yet who have been thrown into confusion by teachers who confidently assert that this is not enough for effective living in God's world. Not enough? Then the Christ of the visiting teachers is not the true Lord as preached by Paul. They must be among those who preach 'another' Christ.[4] For whoever takes seriously the true Christ cannot doubt his adequacy to supply all his people's needs and bring them to their goal. How strange if he who is sufficient to sustain a universe, should be insufficient in power for the little church at Colossae!

Now because of this immeasurable power of Christ described in verses 16 and 17, it is possible to understand and justify the great titles given to him in verse 15. Both descriptions, *the image of the invisible God* and *the first-born of all creation* have caused much discussion, which is explored fully in the larger commentaries. The position taken here is that they both refer to the fact that the power of Almighty God, maker of heaven and earth, *has been manifested* to us through Christ his Son, and *will be manifested* through Christ in the future.

First, Christ is *the image of the invisible God*. The interpretation here must be governed by the fact that the glory of the *invisible* God has actually been manifested to people through Christ. This must therefore refer to the incarnation (Jn. 1 : 14–18). Here the Creator manifested himself through the man Christ Jesus.

The life and ministry of the Lord Jesus was a constant manifestation of the power of the Creator, as demonstrated for example by his miracles (*e.g.* Mk. 4:41). There is nothing strange or incredible in this, for he himself is the agent of all creation (hence the link between verse 15 and verses 16 and 17). Jesus is none other than the Creator entering his creation, so that he has only to speak and it is done (*e.g.* Mk. 3:5); also his word of command has creative power to produce obedience even from the dead (*e.g.* Mk. 5:41). Later we shall see how Christ is able to renew the lost and marred image of God in man (3:10).

Secondly, Christ is *the first-born of all creation*. The context forbids any interpretation of these words that makes Christ first among created beings. It is perverse to say this of one who 'is

[4] *Cf.* 2 Cor. 11:4.

before all things', and through whom all things were made.[5] The simplest explanation is the best; the 'first-born' son was always *the father's heir*. God's Son, Jesus Christ, is 'heir of all things' as the corresponding passage in Hebrews plainly says.[6] This parallel description is relevant here, for it seems to arise out of a similar need to demonstrate the superiority of the Son over all angelic powers.[7]

The created order exists *for* Christ. One day the Heir will enter visibly into his full inheritance before a watching world. On that great day, when Christ's glory manifestly appears, the church will share his inheritance and glory (3 : 3).

It is difficult to believe that these two titles are not related to the situation that had arisen in Colossae. It seems likely, as we shall see later, that the new teachers laid great emphasis on the need for the world actually to *see* in the church the 'manifest power' of God. Paul's answer is that the church's real life is 'hidden' at present with Christ: like her master she will often now appear weak, despised and rejected. If we wish to see the 'manifest glory' of God, we must *look back* to the life and work of the historical Jesus. Or we must *look forward*, because one day this beloved Son will 'appear' again with manifest glory. These two 'appearings', or times of divine manifestation, are constantly celebrated together in Scripture.[8] Meanwhile the church lives between them in time, and the characteristic hallmark of her life is more likely to be suffering than glory.[9]

b. Christ and the church
Supreme over the created order, Christ is now acclaimed as

[5] The persistent visitors from the Jehovah's Witnesses resemble the Arians of the fourth century (in heresies there is nothing new) by denying the eternal nature of the Son of God, and therefore the doctrine of the Trinity. For them Jesus had a beginning of existence, even if he is the highest of created beings. Obviously the phrase 'first-born of all creation' is a superficially convincing proof-text for their position, *taken out of its context*. The context, however, asserts that Christ is 'the creator of the creatures' to use Athanasius's phrase. It would be extraordinary if Paul were guilty of such inconsistency as to make or allow mutually contradictory statements about Christ in the same paragraph. The peril of proof-texts, however, should not deter the Christian from knowing in detail the numerous New Testament passages on which Christian faith in Christ as the eternal Son of God is based. All Christians should be able to demonstrate from Scripture that only witnesses to Jesus are now the true witnesses to Jehovah.

[6] Heb. 1 : 2.   [7] Heb. 1 : 6.   [8] *E.g.* Tit. 2 : 11–13.   [9] Rom. 8 : 18f.

supreme head of the church. This is God's 'new creation'. How foolish therefore to imagine that Paul is here narrowing his horizons and speaking of a smaller 'religious' department within the whole world! The church is the new humanity. The NEB version of 2 Corinthians 5 : 17 well expresses the force of this even with respect to an individual conversion: 'When anyone is united to Christ, there is a new world; the old order has gone, and a new order has already begun.'

When Christ is called *the beginning, the first-born from the dead*, the reference is to his resurrection. This means even more, however, than that he became 'the first to rise from the dead' (as in one of Paul's discourses, Acts 26:23) to be followed by an innumerable company at the general resurrection. It also means that he is now the 'Author of life' (as in one of Peter's sermons, Acts 3 : 15), that is, the one who gives the new life in the Spirit to all God's people. The church therefore is the company of those who share the risen life of Christ. The Christians at Colossae well knew that, before the gospel came to them, they were *dead* in sins, but now God has made them *alive* together with Christ (2 : 13).

It is this basic truth that is enforced by Paul's famous description of Christ as *the head of the body*. The emphasis here is not on the mutual dependence of the various members of the body on one another (but see 2 : 19) so much as on the total dependence of the local (and universal) church on Christ for the continuance of its life. If a body does not hold fast to its head it can hardly hope to survive! Yet it is this striking way of speaking that Paul is to use later with strong intent in 2 : 19. Apparently it is very possible for a church *not* to hold fast to Christ as head, and thus to cut itself off from the essential nourishment that makes for proper growth. Our present passage implies that this will happen when Christ is not given the *pre-eminent* place that is rightfully his. This unique word takes up the idea of *primacy* which has already met us through the 'first-born' of verse 15, repeated in this verse (18). This must mean that the essential primacy of the church belongs to Christ. Submission to any other 'primacy' (*i.e.* such as has been demanded historically by the See of Rome) cannot be required of any churches as a condition of divine nourishment, unity and growth.

In the context of Colossians it must have been clear to the apostle that the new teachers were claiming too much authority. They evidently wished to 'head-up' the work at Colossae and be the unchallenged fount of wisdom and instruction. Authoritarian leadership of this kind is always dangerous for the churches; it can too easily mean that they lose their hold on their heavenly leader. As in the Old Testament story, we in New Testament times can desire a king whom we can see and honour. When the church takes its mind and heart away from Christ and his words, human authority and tradition fills the vacuum. The ultimate consequences of this could be sterility rather than the constant increase and renewal of 2:19.

c. God with us in Christ (verse 19)

Verse 19 concerns the coming of God to dwell with men, foreshadowed from the earliest days of the exodus by the tent in the wilderness.[10] Now it is in Christ that *the fullness of God is pleased to dwell*.

As we have seen, 'fullness' is a characteristic word of the Colossian letter; as a concept it played a large part in second-century Gnosticism, and even at this early stage was evidently becoming a major theme of the visiting teachers. Now the word 'fullness' (*plēroma*) can mean a *supplement*, that is, something added to supply a deficiency,[11] or it can mean a *complement*, that is the full number that makes up a whole, for example a ship's company. The distinction between the two meanings may help to clarify the difference between the apostolic teaching and the new teaching. For Paul there was nothing whatever of the Godhead that was not in Christ; the full complement of divine attributes is to be found in him. But for the new teachers, union with Christ did not of itself bring anyone into such fullness of divine life; there was still room (and need) for a supplementary work of God. This could be thought of by saying that God had still more of himself to give than Christ, or that Christ was not received in all his fullness at conversion. However this was thought of, for Paul it represented a serious misunderstanding. The work of the teacher is to lead people to find their fullness in Christ alone: *he does not possess anything beyond Christ to give to his people*.

The aorist infinitive ('to take up his dwelling') gives verse 19 a reference to the incarnation that is hard to deny.[12] But the present tense in 2:9 ('in him the whole fullness... *dwells* bodily') reminds us that the Christ of history is now at God's right hand.

---

[10] Ex. 25.   [11] Scott, p. 25.   [12] *Cf.* Jn. 1:14.

Incarnation (verse 19) prepares the way for atonement (verse 20), but now we are to seek the fullness of God in Christ *above*, and not on earth (3:1f.)

In the developed Gnosticism of the second century it was axiomatic that a holy God could have no direct dealings with the material world which was thought of as necessarily evil. As a result, numerous gradations of spiritual beings were considered necessary to span the all but infinite gulf between God and man. Whatever ideas of this sort were circulating in the Lycus valley in Paul's day, it was inevitable that even the Christians would be influenced by them (in no age are Christians uncontaminated by the pagan thought-forms of their day). The new teaching brought by the visitors undoubtedly included something of this pagan colouring; it is possible, for instance, that they spoke of additional mediatorial powers assisting in the supreme work of bringing the fullness of God's wisdom, love and power, to the sinful.

Over against these rather 'natural' ideas, the startling words of Paul affirm that it was God's pleasure to make Christ the permanent dwelling place of his divine fullness, so that he should be the one mediator between heaven and earth. The apostolic teaching always takes with the utmost seriousness both the full deity and the complete and perfect humanity of Christ, for only so can he be the sufficient mediator between God and man. This apostolic view forbids a devotion to a human Jesus who is not Christ the Lord, just as it rules out the idea of a 'spiritual' Christ known chiefly as a miracle-worker rather than as a suffering servant.

When I was making final revision of this paragraph, *The Myth of God Incarnate*, a symposium edited by John Hick,[13] had attracted considerable attention. Probably not many who know of the stir caused by this book will have read it (a difficult task for anyone), but the immediate impression given by the imprecise title is not far wrong. The re-interpretation of the doctrine of the incarnation attempted by Maurice Wiles and John Hick turns out to be an abandonment of the truth as formulated in the Nicene Creed (AD 325) and the Chalcedonian Definition (AD 451). One thing the book does not make clear is what view the authors hold of God, an important point if we are trying to understand what is meant by saying that in Christ God became man. If we are

[13] SCM Press, 1977.

pantheists, and identify the universe with God, there will be no difficulty in calling Christ divine, for the same could be said of anyone. But pantheism is incompatible with theism in which a clear distinction between Creator and creature is made. If this contrast between man and his Maker is true, as Christian theism has always affirmed, then the doctrine of the incarnation makes a claim for Christ that has been made for no other human being.

By itself verse 19 is striking enough as a description of a unique and unrepeatable act of divine condescension, but it is only by seeing this verse *in its context* that the full implications of what Paul is saying become clear. It is the fullness of the Almighty God who is Maker of heaven and earth that was pleased to dwell in Christ. What this paragraph demonstrates is that such a belief in Jesus as God incarnate was an essential part of the earliest Christian message.

d. God for us in Christ (verse 20)

If verse 19 tells us that *nothing* of God's fullness is lacking in Christ, verse 20 asserts that *nothing* in the universe is outside the range of God's reconciling work in Christ. Once more, the little word 'all' is significant in both verses.

The need for reconciliation between God and his creation implies, of course, an already existing state of strife and disharmony. A gigantic rupture has taken place, dislocating the relationship between God and man, and throwing into disarray the whole created order. The world knows no settled peace. Futility and decay are the hallmarks of creation (Rom. 8:18f.); hostility and evil are the hallmarks of mankind (verse 21).

The ancient world knew what it was to ask questions about the baffling problems of reconciliation. But without the truth of the gospel there was no possibility of an answer so comprehensive, unqualified and decisive, as Paul gives here. It is not from man but God that the initiative has come: it is not through numberless emissaries that the work has been done but 'through him', the one Christ: the impossibility, as men saw it then, of reconciliation between heaven and earth has found its solution, not in some 'other-worldly drama' (Lohse) but precisely at a certain place, and at a time well remembered, where Christ had endured a bloody and painful death on a Roman cross.

The essence of verse 20 may be summarized by four statements.

(i) *Reconciliation is a work of God.* The Bible is not the story of man's search for God. From the first sentence ('In the beginning God created ...') Holy Scripture is marked out from other religious writings by its unique insistence that the initiative belongs wholly to God. If verse 21 realistically describes man's moral and spiritual state there can be no hope of peace unless God undertakes the work of peacemaking. Verse 19 precedes verse 20 precisely to make clear that God must even take human flesh to provide the Man who will be able to represent all men. So it is only 'through Christ' that reconciliation can be attempted and accomplished.[14]

(ii) *Reconciliation is a work that has been accomplished.* Man need not wait for reconciliation until the end of time, for peace *has been made* by the death of Christ. Therefore reconciliation with God waits not upon human achievement but upon human acceptance.[15] This apostolic affirmation cannot be surrendered in the face of liberal Christianity with its oft-repeated claim that the only change necessary for reconciliation with God lies in the heart of man: God, it is confidently said, does not need to be reconciled to us.

If this were so, the work of Christ in dying would be directed only towards man (to melt his heart and shame him from his foolish rebellion). But it is undeniable, if we take seriously the language of the New Testament, that the work of Christ on the cross was directed toward God. 'We have an advocate with the Father, Jesus Christ the rightenous, and he is the propitiation for our sins.'[16]

Propitiation in the New Testament does not deny the love of God, as in pagan religions, but rather demonstrates it. We need an advocate with the Father, just because he is also our Judge. We have an advocate with the Father, just because, in great mercy, God has come in Christ to provide one.

The Christian doctrine of reconciliation is free from all pagan misrepresentations in that the one who requires to be reconciled is the one who carries out the work of reconciliation. 'In Christ God was reconciling the world to himself.'[17] Once again verse 19 is an essential introduction to verse 20.

The importance of this will be realized when we see that if no objective work of reconciliation was done by Christ's death, the

---

[14] *Cf.* the parallel passage in 2 Cor. 5:17–21, especially verse 18.
[15] *Cf.* the important Rom. 5:11.   [16] 1 Jn. 2:2.   [17] 2 Cor. 5:19.

message of the cross ceases to be a gospel (that is, good news) and becomes simply an appeal.

(iii) *Reconciliation was achieved at the cross.* The 'blood' of the cross means Christ's sacrificial death.[18] The Christian gospel concerns what happened there. The heart of the church's message must therefore be the preaching of 'Christ and him crucified.'[19] The church has constantly to return to this 'word of the cross' to rediscover her gospel, *and her power.* Since presumably the principalities and powers know full well the place of their defeat (2:15), it must be their overriding concern to lead the church to espouse a 'different gospel.'[20] The serpent's shrewdest efforts are aimed to take people's minds off the place where his head was struck a mortal blow. In the case of the Colossian visitors it seems likely that Christ's cross was not the centre of their teaching. Perhaps they were tempted, as we are, to shift the centre of gravity from the historical faith, and to locate the place of power in their own ministry. Paul never locates power in persons or ceremonies. He would turn our eyes back to the cross for the place of power, and up to the throne for the true man of power.

(iv) *Reconciliation through Christ takes in all things.* Finally, the scope of this reconciliation is universal. It takes in the whole created order. 'All things' will share the wonders of peace with God. Other passages fill in the time scale of this, showing how creation must 'wait' for the day when God's sons will be revealed.[21]

What is particularly important here is that Christ is again put before the Colossians, and ourselves, as a *sufficient* Saviour. Nothing and nobody lies outside the scope of his reconciling work. That is not the same as saying that everyone will be saved (an impossible hope if we take Christ's warnings as seriously as his promises). But it is to say that all who are ultimately reconciled to God will be saved by Christ's blood. Paul's statement here is the death knell of syncretism, that most popular of modern heresies, which calls upon men of different faiths to join hands against the common enemies of atheism and materialism. Christians have always confessed that there is but one God; they have also found themselves in loyalty bound to confess that there is but one way to

---

[18] Leon Morris, *The Cross in the New Testament* (Eerdmans, 1965: Paternoster, 1976), p. 219.
[19] 1 Cor. 2:1-5.   [20] 2 Cor. 11:1-6.   [21] Rom. 8:19.

that God, the God-man Christ Jesus. He alone is the God-given mediator. God has made him the agent of reconciliation for *all* just because there is no other mediator capable of reconciling *any*. 'He is the propitiation for our sins: and not for ours only, but also for the sins of the whole world.'[22]

[22] 1 Jn. 2:2 AV.

Colossians 1:21-23
Stable and steadfast

AND you, who once were estranged and hostile in mind, doing evil deeds, [22]*he has now reconciled in his body of flesh by his death, in order to present you holy and blameless and irreproachable before him,* [23]*provided that you continue in the faith, stable and steadfast, not shifting from the hope of the gospel which you heard, which has been preached to every creature under heaven, and of which I, Paul, became a minister.*

This lovely little paragraph is characteristic of New Testament life and experience. The early Christians delighted to speak of the great change brought about for them by the gospel. The contrast between what 'once we were' and what 'now by grace we are' was frequently on their lips in testimony. Here, however, we are not listening to a Colossian Christian testifying to Paul, but to Paul testifying to the Colossians about what had happened to them. As earlier in the chapter (verses 12-14), the apostle thinks it wise to remind them what great things Christ had done for them.

Of course he does this in order to provide for them an illustration, drawn from their own undeniable experience, of the truth of reconciliation. What he has been expounding is no unproven theory, but truth they have been able to verify in life.

Yet we may be sure that there is more to Paul's purpose than this. The contrast between what they once were (verse 21) and the position they now enjoy (verse 22) is painted in such vivid colours, that it looks very much as if the apostle wishes to give the Colossians a new appreciation of the full extent of Christ's reconciling work for them.

Since this particular aim of Paul's will reveal itself several times in this letter, it is worth understanding it clearly now. If the new teachers were the precursors of those who, down the years, have sought in various ways to 'complete' the justifying work of God's saving grace in people's lives, we know that one effect of their teaching is to diminish the importance of the initial experience of conversion. Many teachers of a 'second experience' come to see this further initiation as the really significant change in a person's life bringing them fully into fellowship. Initiation into Christ and the forgiveness of sins, vital as they are, become merely introductory, and the vast mass of believing people are seen as still in this comparatively impoverished position (this latter phrase well describes the historic Roman Catholic position towards Protestant churches, though recently modified). They are Christians, of course, but the real discoveries of God's resources lie ahead of them, and indeed may never be made.

That something like this was happening at Colossae is suggested by the extraordinary emphasis laid by Paul throughout this letter on the unique value and significance of that great spiritual change which people call variously by such words as conversion, justification, regeneration and reconciliation, and which is marked by Christian baptism. For Paul baptism is unrepeatable just because the divine work it signifies is unrepeatable. In a word, incorporation into Christ is always regarded by Paul to be *incomparable*. It is to enter a new world, and become a citizen of a new commonwealth: but of this we shall hear more later (3:10-12).

This paragraph may be divided for ease of study as follows, the 'you' referring directly to the Colossians, and indirectly to all Christian people.

1. What you once were (verse 21)
2. Where you now stand (verse 22)
3. How you must go on (verse 23)

1. What you once were (verse 21)

In view of Ephesians 2:12 this reference to estrangement from God suggests that the Colossian Christians had formerly been Gentiles. A 'hostile mind' toward God was no Gentile preserve, however, as the crucifixion proved. Such are the appalling consequences of the fall, that all people everywhere are known by a mentality that is naturally antagonistic to the truth of God. The unbeliever's normal reaction to the view that this verse takes of him will often prove the point. Antagonistic, please note, not merely apathetic. We deceive ourselves if we imagine that human apathy is the problem, and not, deep down, an enmity which resists the claims of God.[1] Fallen man is not therefore 'good at heart', if Jesus is to be believed.[2] 'Evil deeds' are the inevitable result of an evil heart, and persist in every human culture and reappear in every new generation, presenting man in society with his most intractable problems.

Such is the stark and grim description Paul gives of what the Colossians once were, and there is no reason to think that they would have dissented from the verdict, any more than an enlightened Christian would wish to disagree today.

2. Where you now stand (verse 22)

From the desperate position of verse 21 the Colossians have been rescued. Now they enjoy peace with God. Through Christ's death, they stand in God's presence *holy and blameless and irreproachable*.

An important question here is whether Paul is using the language of justification (this would refer to their standing, as accepted by God into his family), or of sanctification (this would refer to their actual state, as people of exceptional moral excellence). Distinguished commentators are found on either side. The context suggests that the language used points to the former, though Calvin who agrees with this, goes on to show the 'inseparable connection' between justification and sanctification here. In those who are 'reconciled', the work of perfecting the saints has already begun. At the last day blameless and irreproachable holiness will indeed be ours.[3] The reasons for interpreting verse 22 as descriptive of justification, however, are strong ones.

a. Reconciliation is something God has achieved through Christ once and for all. The Colossians have no part in that achievement but to accept it thankfully. They are *now reconciled*.

b. The place where this great change took place was at *the*

---

[1] *Cf.* Jn. 8:10; Rom. 5:10; Jas. 4:4.   [2] Mk. 7:21-23.
[3] Calvin, p. 159.

cross, and not in their hearts. It is an act right outside themselves that made them 'holy people'. (The emphasis on 'flesh' and 'death' is deliberately strong to counter the emerging mystical and Gnostic tendencies: no 'tuning into the Infinite' for apostolic Christianity except through the harsh discords of the cross).

c. Lohse points out that the verb *to present* was used in legal language, meaning 'to bring another before the court'.[4] Brought before the divine Judge the now reconciled Christian is found to be without reproach, stain or fault. Despite past estrangement it is possible for the new believer immediately to live his life in God's presence. This is the language of justification.

What a contrast this is! What a change of position! Can anything be remotely comparable to this transference from darkness to light? And as has been said, this change of position is always accompanied by a change of heart. The reconciled man is a new man in Christ. Now he loves and reverences the God he formerly distrusted. And he who loves the Lord comes to hate evil.

3. How you must go on (verse 23)

This verse confirms our understanding of Paul's meaning. The position the Colossians occupy before God as 'acceptable people' depends upon one condition—continuance in the faith. This continuance is then defined as faithfulness to the gospel. The gospel is then defined as:

(i) the gospel they had already heard, *i.e.* which had already proved itself to be living and powerful;

(ii) the gospel the world was also hearing, *i.e.* which had already proved itself 'catholic' or universal;

(iii) the gospel Paul had received and served, *i.e.* which had already proved itself to be apostolic.

The duty of the Colossians to this gospel is expressed in fine words, whose precise meaning epitomizes the appeal of the whole Colossian letter.

a. They are to be *stable*, literally, established or well-founded in the truth. To move from the gospel is to move from the foundations on which Christ has built his church, and therefore to lose Christian 'stability'.

b. They are to be *steadfast*. This is the great call of 1 Cor-

---

[4]Lohse, p. 65, a most illuminating discussion.

inthians 15:58, where apostolic truth was again at stake. It means loyalty to the truths by which they were saved.[5]

c. They are not to *shift.* A unique New Testament word, it literally means that they are not to be *dissuaded* from the hope of the gospel. This is extremely significant language, specially characteristic perhaps of the captivity epistles.[6] The chief blessing of the gospel is the hope it contains for the future. Meanwhile, in the present, the church lives by faith. Now we have a 'taste' of 'the powers of the world to come'.[7] It may be that the new teachers urged the believers not to be content with this 'taste', but to claim from God the full heavenly feast. But this, for Paul, is to 'shift from the hope'. It is to refuse to walk by faith. It is to bring Christ down to earth. It is to give oneself to 'another' gospel.

To *continue in the faith* is to be content with the gospel that first saved and delivered us from spiritual death and estrangement with God, and brought us straightaway to live in his presence, at peace with him. It is to base our lives and our teaching upon the apostolic doctrines of grace. It is for those whose confidence that they are reconciled is in Christ's work *for* us, not in Christ's work *in* us. It is to be unmoved and immoveable in the face of strong winds of new doctrine, not just when people would deny the apostolic gospel but when, more subtly, they would improve upon it. For the sixteenth-century Anglican Reformers it was the rediscovery of the 'finished work' of Christ on the cross as an atonement for the sins of the world that made the medieval Mass so intolerable to them. From experience they knew that the focus of the worshippers' attention was on the words and actions of the priest at the altar; there is concrete evidence of this in the new consecration prayer prepared for the Holy Communion service in the Book of Common Prayer. The words of this prayer vigorously turn our attention back to *what Christ did* by his death at Golgotha, 'who made there ... a full, perfect, and sufficient sacrifice ... for the sins of the whole world'. Notice the emphatic *there* as opposed to *here*. Communicants are then invited to listen to *what Christ said* at the institution of the supper, since it is not the mysteriously powerful words of the priest that matter but rather the words Christ spoke by way of explanation for this remembrance of his passion. It is these words that must reach every listening ear and lodge in every worshipper's mind and heart.

[5] 1 Cor. 15:2.   [6] *Cf.* Eph. 1:18.   [7] Heb. 6:5.

Today the situation is confused for many Christian people. Frequently one meets 'catholic' believers who claim with obvious sincerity that they believe and trust in Christ's once-for-all sacrifice for sins. Shall we not say, therefore, that the old misunderstandings have been removed and that all believers can reasonably look forward to meeting with one heart and mind at the Lord's table? Only if we can all agree that the *finality* of the sacrifice on the cross is a cardinal tenet of the New Testament, not only here in Colossians (1:20, 22) but also in the letter to the Hebrews where the imagery is very telling. Christ is pictured as having sat down at the right hand of the Father, his work of offering sacrifice completed, while his presence at the place of honour witnesses to the fact that he is (and therefore those that are 'in him' are also) now accepted fully, finally and for ever (Heb. 10:1-18).

It must reluctantly be said that this finality is still contradicted by much Catholic principle and practice even since Vatican II. Granted that the Mass is no independent or additional sacrifice, it remains for many a 'real' sacrifice, that is, the same sacrifice which Christ offered, though offered now in a different way. But why is this constant 'renewal' of Christ's sacrifice necessary, even if it is offered in a bloodless manner? The official answer remains unchanged, as in paragraph 29 of Paul VI's encyclical *Mysterium Fidei* (1965):

> Instructed by the Lord and the Apostles, the Church has always offered it not only for the sins, punishments, satisfactions and needs of the faithful still alive, but also for those who have died in Christ but are not yet fully cleansed.[8]

Notice carefully the final phrase 'not yet fully cleansed'. But this *full* cleansing of all sin is precisely what Christ by his bloody sacrifice has won for his people. This is the glory of the cross (1:27); this is the hope of the gospel from which we may not shift (1:23); from the enjoyment of this 'freedom from sin' we cannot allow ourselves to be recaptured by the chains of 'religion' (2:8-15). To those with a heart for this spiritual freedom the official Roman Catholic doctrine of the Mass remains intolerable still.

[8]Quoted by H. M. Carson in *Dawn or Twilight?* (IVP, 1976), p. 115.

Paul's teaching remains the only road to spiritual 'assurance', a much neglected aspect of Christian truth: indeed it has often been regarded as peculiarly evangelical. Writing of the Seventh Earl of Shaftesbury, Georgina Battiscombe says that

> No existing record suggests that at any period of his life did Ashley experience that sudden and definite assurance of salvation which is the classic Evangelical conversion. If he in fact ever had such an experience it most probably would have been during his childhood under the influence of Maria Millis.[9]

But sudden or gradual, can there be an intelligent and genuine turning to Christ without 'that definite assurance of salvation'? Alas, it seems that there can, but only because believers do what Paul here forbids and shift from the hope (*i.e.* assurance) of the gospel by seeking something more than Christ crucified as the sufficient foundation for their soul's confidence. Assurance of ultimate salvation is God's intention for every Christian (1 Jn. 5:13), and, incidentally despite his most recent biographer's hesitations, Shaftesbury certainly enjoyed it. The celebrated minister of St Peter's, Dundee, Robert Murray M'Cheyne, wrote these words about such Christian certainty:

> My hope is built on nothing less
> Than Jesus' blood and righteousness;
> I dare not trust the sweetest frame,
> But wholly lean on Jesus' name.
> On Christ, the solid Rock, I stand;
> All other ground is sinking sand.

[9]G. Battiscombe, *Shaftesbury* (Constable, 1974), p. 99.

Colossians 1:24-29
Apostolic ministry

NOW I rejoice in my sufferings for your sake, and in my flesh I complete what is lacking in Christ's afflictions for the sake of his body, that is, the church, ²⁵of which I became a minister according to the divine office which was given to me for you, to make the word of God fully known, ²⁶the mystery hidden for ages and generations but now made manifest to his saints. ²⁷To them God chose to make known how great among the Gentiles are the riches of the glory of this mystery, which is Christ in you, the hope of glory. ²⁸Him we proclaim, warning every man and teaching every man in all wisdom, that we may present every man mature in Christ. ²⁹For this I toil, striving with all the energy which he mightily inspires within me.

Already the nature of Paul's appeal to the Colossians is taking shape. It is a plea for continuance in the truth of the apostolic gospel. In a word, it is a demand for loyalty.

But loyalty to Paul's gospel cannot be separated from loyalty to himself, and his apostolic office. This is the explanation for the magnificent section before us. In it the Colossians are invited to examine the apostle's calling, the shape of his ministry and the aims he felt compelled to pursue, as well as to recognize the genuine signs of God at work in the man himself.

It is not in character for Paul to indulge in such an apologia for its own sake. He consistently refused to preach himself.[1] While this may give us added confidence in the apostle, it is ironic that his dislike for self-advertisement cost him dearly in his own day.

[1] 2 Cor. 4:5.

Astonishing as it may be to those who know him by his letters, he appears to have cut a poor figure in the estimate of many contemporaries, some of whom did not hestitate to say so.[2]

His duty to defend and justify his ministry was necessary here for local reasons. It seems almost certain that the new teaching at Colossae attracted favourable notice largely because of the compelling ministry of its leading advocates. We know, for instance, that among them were persuasive speakers of great charm (2:4). By comparison with such impressive ministry, the work of Epaphras, at least, seemed somewhat pedestrian. We note that Paul thinks it necessary to repeat his commendation of Epaphras in verses 12 and 13 of chapter 4. The 'I can assure you that he has worked hard for you' of the LB version neatly catches the sense one gets that Epaphras lacked showy gifts, and that, because of this, he had critics in Colossae only too ready to disparage him.

What then is a God-given ministry? What is authentic service, which we may recognize as such? It was important for the Colossians, as it is for us, to have some standards by which to measure the claims people make for themselves, and by which true spiritual leadership may be known in the churches. The permanent value of this great passage is that it provides the church in every generation with just such a standard.

Some kind of analysis is needed for the study of a paragraph so full of significant words and themes. The plan here suggested attempts to show the beautiful balances in Paul's description: but the twofold divisions are not meant to imply that there is more than one ministry. We head straight for trouble whenever we separate what God has joined.

1. *The twofold ministry*
   a. A servant of the gospel, to make the word of God fully known
   b. A servant of the church, to make the people of God fully mature
2. *The twofold proclamation*
   a. Christ in you ...
   b. ... the hope of glory
3. *The twofold qualification*

[2] 2 Cor. 10:10.

a. Fellowship in Christ's sufferings (hardships)
b. Fellowship in Christ's resurrection (toil)

1. The twofold ministry

Ministry means service. Paul's apostolic ministry was his particular calling to be a servant of God. The form taken by that service is finely brought out by a little phrase twice used in this section, 'of which I became a minister', referring to *the gospel* (verse 23) and to *the church* (verses 24, 25). Paul knew himself called to serve the word of God: he also knew himself called to serve the people of God.

This twofold call is not to different, or even to complementary, ministries, as though Paul with his capacities might take on both, while other less gifted mortals must select one or other aspect of Christian ministry. For it is precisely by teaching the Word of God that the church of God is to be served. It is by the truth of the gospel that the church is formed, sustained and equipped. Without a satisfactory ministry of the Word, the church must either wither and die, or assume more or less grotesque forms.

This primary ministry governs all other forms of ministry in the churches. No spiritual ministries can exist safely or fruitfully in isolation from the 'Word', without risk of becoming both meaningless and lifeless. For example, the sixteenth-century Reformers rediscovered the power and significance of the *ministry of the sacraments* just because they rediscovered the primacy of the ministry of the Word. In our own day, we can properly secure a *ministry of the Spirit*, much to be desired in an enfeebled church, only through a ministry of the Word, as vividly shown throughout the Acts of the Apostles.[3]

This then is Paul's great aim. He wants fully to dispense this truth in such a way that every Christian man and woman is led towards spiritual maturity.

But we may ask how this aim differed from that of the new teachers. What is behind these emphatic statements of Paul? An answer to this may be found in the use of the word 'mystery' which controls the central part of the paragraph (verses 26, 27).

Some (*e.g.* Abbott)[4] see nothing particularly significant in

---

[3] *E.g.* Acts 2:14ff.; 4:8ff.; 6:4; 7; through to 28:25–30.
[4] Abbott, p. 233.

Paul's use of this word, pointing out how it was the ordinary, and colloquial, term for 'a secret'. Paul uses it to emphasize, not that the gospel truths are 'mysterious', but that they are undiscoverable by man, and have been disclosed by God. Therefore it is a normal word for him to use when stressing the essential character of the Christian faith as 'revelation.'[5]

But there may be more to it than that. Paul and his friends at Colossae lived in a world of 'mystery' religions, all offering in their different ways rites of initiation that would bring seekers into the privileged circle of those few who had found the 'secret' of life and existence. Now Paul's word 'mystery' comes from the same root as the verb 'to initiate', and 'in the vocabulary of religion it stands for the whole complex of initiation, cult, and secret doctrine on which the numerous private religious brotherhoods of the time were based.[6]

Of course Paul is not saying that the visitors were peddling such spurious wares as the pagan cultists. But he does seem to suggest that they are perilously close to occupying similar ground in their 'Christian' teaching. They spoke of truths 'hidden' from the generality of Christian people; they seem to have offered a supplementary rite of circumcision as a kind of second baptism (2:11); they described this spiritual treasure in glowing terms as bringing people a 'glory' hitherto not known; and they claimed that they alone had the power to bring people this experience of perfection.

Paul's understanding of the 'mystery' is quite different from this. It is acknowledged that the truth had been 'hidden' in ages past, but is hidden no longer. Now it is known by *all* God's people (verse 26). The glory of this mystery lies not in its exclusiveness, belonging to a few, but in its inclusiveness, for it is intended for the nations (well brought out in Eph. 3:6 where the solidarity of Jews and Gentiles in Christ is boldly described). This 'mystery' is nothing more nor less than the gospel of Christ: and it is brought to people not by semi-secret rites but by public proclamation. The power of its ministers lies in their work of instruction, correction and training. It is true that this 'mystery' involves a satisfying and present experience for the heart (Christ in you) but its glory lies in its gift of hope for the future (verse 27). Its benefits are not for some believers, a spiritual elite, but for everyone in Christ (verse 28).

[5] Rom. 16:25; Eph. 3:9.   [6] Beare, p. 180.

Paul's use of the word 'mystery' therefore is not intended so much to compare the gospel with the pagan mystery cults, as to compare his own ministry with that of the new teachers. Now the outstanding characteristic of his ministry is that of authoritative and comprehensive teaching. The goal he has set himself is to bring all of God's truth to all of God's people. This is unforgettably expressed in verses 25 and 28.

a. To make the word of God fully known
b. To make the people of God fully mature

a. To make the word of God fully known

It is quite unlikely that verse 25 expresses Paul's ambition to complete the preaching of the gospel to the known world.[7] It is better understood in context as an expression of Paul's determination to give God's people the fullest gospel—the whole Christian message. This meets the claim of the visitors who had had the temerity to say that Epaphras had not preached the whole truth to the Colossians.

To preach Christ is to preach the full truth, and verse 27 eloquently describes just how full of spiritual treasure and glory this gospel is. But the Christ we preach must be the full Christ as taught by the apostles (*e.g.* 1:15-20). This is to say that people cannot know Christ better without knowing the Scriptures better. It is only through an expository ministry that the Word of God can be fully known: and it is only through the Word of God that Christ can be fully known. There is no short cut here for busy (?lazy) pastors or impatient (?undisciplined) believers. Such Bible teaching and Bible study is the crying need of the church today.

b. To make the people of God fully mature

Verse 28 gives a sobering insight into the extent of Paul's labours. He stands revealed as more than a public preacher; he is also the personal instructor, giving time and thought to individuals.[8] The phrase 'every man' repeated three times so markedly, is evidently intended to rule out any idea of a church within a church, composed of those who alone are able to benefit from deeper truths. Maturity is the goal for all God's people.

[7] Rom. 15:19f.   [8] *Cf.* the important Acts 20:20.

Lohse has an instructive note on 'perfection' as understood in the Hellenistic world of Paul's day, where, apparently, it often referred to those who were filled with experiences of divine power and wisdom. 'To such a conception Col(ossians) contrasts its own understanding of wisdom and perfection which is wholly directed toward obedient fulfilment of the Divine will.'[9]

To achieve his purposes of proclaiming Christ to everyone, Paul describes his ministry in two complementary ways. Negatively, he *warns* the young believers, correcting and admonishing them as it is necessary: positively, he *teaches* them the whole counsel of God. This is one more example of Paul's balanced view of ministry. Neither aspect of pastoral instruction can be neglected without loss. Paul did not shrink, as we are tempted to do, from the uncongenial work of rebuking error and evil. In a fallen world where people naturally go astray, and especially where the church is marked by unfaithfulness, such 'negative' teaching, as it is sometimes called, cannot be avoided. By warning people against a 'fuller' and therefore a false gospel, Paul actually leads them to rediscover the fullness of the gospel that saved them. By warning them against pseudo-spirituality he guides them along the paths of true maturity. By warning the church of false ministry, he helps the Christians to rediscover the hallmarks of true ministry. Such warnings are therefore essentially positive in intention and result, and they are indispensable to a balanced teaching ministry.

To sustain such a programme as described in verse 28, even in one local church, must normally be beyond the strength of one person, even with the prodigious energies of a Paul (verse 29). It is interesting, therefore, to read later on in this letter (3:16) that all the members of the Christian community at Colossae were expected to take a share in this double ministry by warning and teaching one another. As usual Paul expects all people to receive from him, not only a message, but a ministry.[10]

We ought not to leave Paul's understanding of his ministry without noticing just how genuine his concept of servanthood was. He expresses his sense of dependence on God so plainly in this section (as in a parallel passage in Eph. 3) that we suspect an intentional contrast with other teachers. Assuming that this is not the language of conventional piety, we may summarize his

[9] Lohse, p. 78.   [10] *Cf.* 2 Cor. 5:17-21.

position in terms of three negatives, which together are deeply impressive.

(i) *He had not chosen his task (verse 25)*. Explicitly Paul states that this divine office, or task, *was given* to him for the benefit of the Colossians, among others. By contrast, the ministry of the new teachers was self-chosen. It could be said of them, as of the false prophets in Jeremiah's day, 'I did not send these prophets, yet they went in haste.' [11]

(ii) *He had not imagined his message (verse 25)*. Despite his claims to be an authoritative mouthpiece for Christian truth,[12] Paul never suggests that any part of his message originated from within his own mind and experience. What the Colossians received from him (through Epaphras), he had received from Christ:[13] it was therefore the Word of God (verse 25). By contrast it is implied that the new teachers derived their distinctive themes from sources as varied as human tradition (2:8) and visionary dreams (2:18), but not from God. Once again they stand in succession to the pseudo-teachers of Jeremiah's day. 'I did not speak to them, yet they prophesied.'[14]

(iii) *He had not concealed anything from anyone (verses 26-28)*. Most striking of all in this section is the way in which the pattern of apostolic service is dictated by the example of divine activity. Truths that people could not know because they belonged to the hidden counsels of God cannot be stolen from heaven by the inspired guesses of religious geniuses, and Paul never portrays himself in such a role. Even when caught up into the 'third heaven' he has nothing to tell us of his experiences there (2 Cor. 12:1-4), a strange contrast to human religious traditions!

It is in the fact that God has now disclosed the truth of the 'mystery', that Paul finds the justification for his ministry. What God has *made manifest*, he may make *fully known*; what God *chose to make known*, he may, without presumption, broadcast (this is the force of 'proclaim' in verse 28) from the housetops. What God has given to his people of his truth, belongs now to them.[15] And it is Paul's determination that every Christian should have what rightfully belongs to him. There is no excuse now for impoverished believers: the treasure that is in Christ belongs equally to all. The contrast between this and the

---

[11] Je. 23:21a NEB.   [12] *E.g.* Gal. 1:1-12.   [13] *Cf.* 1 Cor. 15:1-10.
[14] Je. 23:21b.   [15] Dt. 29:29.

philosophy of the new teachers is plainly drawn. According to their assumed superiority, God had revealed the richest things only for a few: worse still, these hidden treasures could not be discovered except through their special ministries. They seemed to disparage the glory of what God had revealed in Christ, and claimed to discover for the Christians treasure that God had not revealed.

To summarize, the great apostle sees himself as having no authority to decide his message, his mission, or his methods of ministry. What God has given, that he teaches, neither more nor less. When God appoints him, he takes up his task. If God chooses to reveal Christ to the nations, there, to everyone, Paul goes. Above all, because the supreme activity of God is to disclose his Word of truth, Paul's supreme activity is as a teacher of truth. To that message, therefore, we may now turn.

2. The twofold proclamation

What is the word of God that Paul proclaimed? What is the open secret? What are the gloriously rich treasures which the apostle gives his life to preach? His answer is extraordinary in its conciseness, yet so characteristic of this letter. The whole matter can be put in a word, or rather a name; *him we proclaim* (verse 28).

We already have a fair idea of what Paul meant by preaching Christ, through what has been called the Great Christology (1:15-20). We shall discover more in Paul's exposition of the crucified Christ in chapter 2 (verses 14-15), and of the returning Christ in chapter 3 (verses 1-4). But the special interest of this paragraph lies in its definition of the 'mystery' as being 'Christ in you, the hope of glory'. Both these phrases are sufficiently unusual to make us aware that Paul, once again, has probably shaped his words to meet the misconceptions that were gaining ground.

a. Christ in you...
Many commentators, and a few translators, have preferred the rendering, 'Christ among you'. Taken in this way, the essential feature of the 'mystery' is the offer of salvation to the Gentile world. That this is a vital element in the new disclosure is undeniable.[16] 'One cannot but feel, however,' as Scott says, 'that

---

[16] *Cf.* Eph. 3:6 and context.

after the solemn manner in which Paul has led up to the disclosure of the secret "mystery" there would be something of an anti-climax if it consisted of nothing more than the inauguration of a Gentile mission.'[17] In any case the 'mystery' is said to be 'the word of God' (verses 25–26), and the content of this is not properly described by the extent of its proclamation. It seems a poor conclusion to verse 27 to say that what is to be made known *among the Gentiles* is, simply, *Christ among you*.

That *Christ in you* is the true rendering is likely just because it is so uncharacteristic of Paul in general, yet so clearly relevant to the theme of this particular letter. Normally Paul describes the Christian as a person *in Christ* (1:2, and compare the reiterated '*in him*' of this letter). Christ is at God's right hand, and Christians share his access to the Father, and his victory over the principalities and powers, by being joined to him. It is the special activity of the third person of the Trinity, the Holy Spirit, to indwell the heart of the believing Christian, as Jesus foretold.[18] So in Paul's use of terminology, when it is a matter of 'God for us', it is of Christ he speaks, and when it is a matter of 'God in us' it is of the Spirit that he usually speaks.[19]

Now it is Paul's teaching that the fullness of God's power and glory resides in the exalted Christ, and that *by faith* Christians are united to the heavenly Lord. But it seems that the walk of faith was being disparaged and something more immediate demanded. Did the new teachers offer something more dynamic, centred not at God's right hand in heaven but in the human heart?

It seems very likely that they were the forerunners of those who have made a false, and ultimately fatal, distinction between God's work *for* us and *in* us. To Paul these were two sides of *the same work of grace*. He may have feared a new outlook where activity of 'God in us' was a further work of grace not irrevocably linked with his activity 'for us'. In that case justification and sanctification, forgiveness and life, would develop into separate gifts of God.

> To wrest these two things apart and make separable gifts of grace of them evinces a confusion in the conception of Christ's salvation which is nothing less than portentous. It forces from us the astonished cry, Is Christ divided? And it compels us to

[17] Scott, p. 34.   [18] Jn. 14:17.
[19] As, characteristically, in 1 Cor. 6:19; 2 Cor. 1:22; Gal. 4:6.

point afresh to the primary truth that we do not obtain the benefits of Christ apart from, but only in and with His Person; and that when we have him we have all.[20]

Paul, however, has no intention of allowing his readers to think that Christ might be divided. Several commentators have noticed that in this Colossian letter, where Paul might normally have spoken of the Holy Spirit, he substitutes the name of Christ. That is what he does here. Is it conceivable that the visitors had suggested that the coming of the Spirit into the heart would bring greater riches than the Christian had hitherto known? But Paul cannot allow this for a moment. The work of the Spirit is precisely to bring within our reach the heavenly blessings of Christ. It is by his power that Christ can be said to dwell in our hearts by faith.[21] The ministry of the Spirit is nothing less (or more) than to bring us to Christ and Christ to us. It is the ministry of the gospel.

Here, then, Paul answers the demand for the richest experience of God that it is permissible for human beings to have. When we have begun to grasp the greatness of Christ, and then grasp the closeness of the union we may have with him, he in us and we in him, we can ask of God no more.

Yet it *is* God's purpose to give us still more. What can this mean?

b. ... The hope of glory

No doubt this was a word of *comfort*. The popularity of the mystery religions was due in part to whatever assurances they could offer of immortality. And the appeal of the visitors may also have been due to a search among the Christians for a greater spiritual certainty. Whatever truth there is in this, we may be sure that the promises of the gospel are greatly supported by the presence of God's love in our hearts.[22] So Paul's customary teaching is that the Spirit within is that personal guarantee of an eternal inheritance which Christians need.[23] It is foolish to speak of this as presumptuous, since *glory* is inconceivable in Paul's gospel apart from *grace*. More than that, it is only on the certainty

---

[20] B. B. Warfield, *Perfectionism* (Presbyterian and Reformed Publishing Company, 1967), p. 357.
[21] *Cf.* the parallel passage in Eph. 3:7-19.
[22] *Cf.* Rom. 5:3-5.   [23] Eph. 1:13-14; 2 Cor. 1:22.

of 'the hope' Christians possess, that faith and love can now be built.

The gospel therefore is good news of a great future. And herein lies a word of *caution*, which is very important to Paul's present purpose. The visitors spoke unguardedly of God doing a still greater work for the Colossians than had been achieved for them so far. By doing this they failed to distinguish between the fruits of Christ's reconciling work that are to be enjoyed now, and those which we come to possess only in the life of the world to come. This dangerous tendency to see the present rather than the future as the time when God's 'full salvation' is to be enjoyed, reappears in various forms in the New Testament, most extremely in the claim of certain teachers in Ephesus that 'the resurrection is past already'.[24] The reason for the ready acceptance of this type of teaching lay in the language of zeal by which it was presented. The unwary could easily come to think that the mark of spirituality was to claim *all* of God's gifts *now*. It is not always easy to understand that part of God's blessings of redemption are to be possessed now, but that other aspects of redemption remain a matter of promise (*e.g.* the redemption of the body we wait for, described in Rom. 8:23).

But it is the language of presumption and folly, not the language of faith, to claim that God has given something which a sober judgment cannot discern in reality. Harry Ironside in a moving section of autobiography in his book, *Holiness, the False and the True*, writes of being caught up in certain second-blessing and faith-healing circles, many years ago, where at first 'the heartfelt testimonies of experiences so remarkable that I could not doubt their genuineness' led him to seek a similar experience of freedom from all sin, and 'the blessing of perfect love'. Not until painful years later did he begin to see 'what a string of derelicts this holiness teaching left in its train. I could count scores of persons who had gone into utter infidelity because of it.' By this time the testimony meetings had become a hindrance rather than a help. 'Sick people testified to being healed by faith, and sinning people declared they had the blessing of holiness!' Finally, and inevitably, 'I found myself becoming cold and cynical. Doubts as to everything assailed me.'[25]

[24] 2 Tim. 2:18.
[25] H. A. Ironside, *Holiness, the False and the True* (Pickering & Inglis, 1959), pp. 15, 24, 28.

76

Such must always be the end of that road for an honest person. If we claim to receive what God has not promised, the result must ultimately be disillusionment.

How different is Paul's gospel! The experience of Christ dwelling in our hearts by faith gives not the possession but the promise of full salvation. The greatest gift of Christ in the present is hope for the future. Since he is in heaven our hopes are inevitably centred there. For this life, grace is sufficient. Glory (Paul's 'second blessing') belongs to the age to come.

In putting together these two phrases, 'Christ in you, the hope of glory', we at last discover the right perspectives of the true gospel. The Christ who is 'in' us, is in heaven: our hope is in heaven. Hence our present walk with God is one of faith, not sight. 'Without having seen him, you love him; though you do not now see him you believe in him and rejoice with unutterable and exalted joy. As the outcome of your faith you obtain the salvation of your souls.'[26] We must not, however, swing to the other extreme. Christianity is more than a hope, however glorious. It is, even now, 'Christ in you'! Full salvation belongs to the last day, but a real salvation belongs to the Christian here and now. If a believer cannot yet say that he is free from the *presence* of sin, he certainly should be able to say that he is free from the *penalty* of sin. And by God's grace, it is his daily privilege to find Christ at work in him saving him from the downward *pull* of sin. It is therefore an unbalanced Christianity which takes either part of this twofold message to the exclusion of the other. Turning for a moment from the sublime to the ridiculous, James Denney used to tell the story of the doctor who fell among brigands, and who, when challenged, 'Your money or your life', replied, 'Gentlemen, I congratulate myself on your moderation; my practice is to take both.' It is good advice! Let us refuse a salvation which polarizes on 'now' or 'then', but rather let us recognize both present and future salvation as our rightful inheritance.

3. The twofold qualification

Two famous verses, one at the beginning of this paragraph (verse 24), and the other at the end (verse 29), remain to be studied. They speak of the sufferings people may receive, and the labours people must give, if a true Christian ministry is to be exercised.

[26] 1 Pet. 1:8–9.

a. Fellowship in Christ's sufferings (hardships)

The clue to solving some of the puzzles set by verse 24 may lie in the tell-tale phrase, 'to complete what is lacking'. Our ears are more attuned now to words and slogans that probably originated with the new teachers, but which Paul turns to his own advantage. Here surely is an echo from the preaching of these eloquent persuaders, for to 'complete what is lacking' was the very *raison d'être* of their mission. And it was not just the rank and file of the church at Colossae who were condemned for lacking the requisite spiritual fullness: their leaders were suspect as well.

It seems likely that Paul is aware of their suspicions of his apostleship as lacking certain hallmarks of spiritual power, and that with deep irony, he points to his sufferings as the guarantee of his authenticity.

The initial difficulty of verse 24 lies in the suggestion that there is something lacking in Christ's sufferings, rather than in Paul's apostleship: and the overlong discussion this can generate draws attention away from the basic theme of the verse. We can say, without fear of contradiction, that the special emphasis in Colossians on the final achievement of the cross in reconciling all things to God, in removing all sins, and making possible the forgiveness of all trespasses, makes it quite impossible to suppose that there is something lacking in the vicarious and atoning sufferings of Christ that must be supplied by the apostle (1:22; 2:14).

We shall be wiser to go back to the time of Paul's conversion for help in appreciating his language here. On that great day he discovered, among other things, two things about suffering that were to mark his entire ministry. First, to his shame and horror, he discovered that he had been persecuting not a handful of troublesome extremists but the Lord of glory.[27] Secondly, he discovered that his chief privilege as Christ's chosen instrument was to be understood in terms of suffering for the sake of the Name.[28] It was a shattering reversal of values. When a persecutor, he had been marked by a 'power' and an 'authority' that all could recognize. But how differently he had left Damascus from the way he entered it![29] Now he who had pursued, was pursued, and he who had inflicted suffering, was to endure it.

Yet he could rejoice in this. How? Only because in such

---

[27] Acts 9:4-5.   [28] Acts 9:15-16.   [29] Acts 9:25.

suffering for the sake of the Name (in Colossians, 'for the sake of the body, the church', another indication of the intimate union between Christ and his people), did he enter into deeper fellowship with Christ in his sufferings.

As in all true fellowship there is a measure of mutual sharing and receiving. This would explain the *double entendre* that seems to exist in the words of this verse. Before his return in glory, the risen Lord will continue to share the afflictions of his people until the full measure of the church's sufferings (which are Christ's afflictions) is made up. Paul's sufferings helped to complete that full toll and hasten the end. But we cannot doubt that Paul sees his own ministry as being 'completed' by this sharing in Christ's sufferings. The phrase 'in my flesh' is particularly telling. The visitors would have said that his lack was of blessings in his 'spirit'. He saw the fullness of his apostolic ministry in the sufferings received in his *flesh*. He can dare to rejoice in such hardships just because his ministry exists for the church's sake, not for his own sake.

This verse, then, is about Paul's suffering and the way in which he discovered their real significance. He rejoices in suffering in no masochistic sense, but just because it is necessary for the sake of those to whom he goes, and finally because it leads him into the richest union with the Lord himself, sharing if possible in Christ's afflictions.[30]

b. Fellowship in Christ's resurrection (toil)

Verse 29 shows Paul to have been a tireless worker. But he ascribes his extraordinary energy to more than a strong constitution. The work described in verse 28 is harder than anyone who has not attempted it can imagine, and might sap the strength of the youngest and fittest of people without the strength which God supplies. The power that Paul looked to for the carrying on of his ministry was that 'working of God' in raising Christ from the dead (2 : 12). It was 'resurrection power'.

Since an offer of 'power' was some part of the prospectus of the new teaching, we may expect Paul to explain his own teaching by way of contrast. We shall get some understanding of the apostolic viewpoint, which is, to say the least, not the most familiar one to modern Christians, by finding, in this remarkable verse, answers to three questions.

[30] *Cf.* Phil. 3 : 10.

(i) *How do we appropriate God's power?* Paul's surprising answer is that we receive it not so much by believing as by *working*. It is when we 'toil and strive' at a God-given task, that we receive God-given energy. If we hope to know in experience the work of God within us 'both to will and to work for his good pleasure' we must first set to *work*.[31] Paul would never have said that 'power for service' is received by faith alone. It can be appropriated only by the faith that works, or to put it another way, by the work that relies on God to energize us as we try to do his bidding. As Paul toiled (a particularly strong word, also used by him to describe his backbreaking manual work, tentmaking)[32] in teaching with strenuous endeavour, God himself granted strength and capacity for the work. God gives his power to workers.

(ii) *How do we experience God's power?* It is easy to think that the believer should have a direct apprehension of so mighty an enduement as the resurrection power of Christ within him. But there is no indication that Paul was immediately conscious of God's strength surging within him. What he was aware of was the sweat of hard labour in the service of the Lord. 'Striving' (Gk. *agōnizomai*) meant that it was agony rather than ecstasy to do this work properly. It looks very unlikely that Paul would have taken with much seriousness our modern questions as to what it 'feels like' to be equipped with spiritual power.

(iii) *How do we recognize God's power?* Here again we easily look for the wrong signs of divine activity. While God is, of course, free to work without using human agents, the normal evidence of God at work is, simply, *his servants at work*. And surely it is evidence enough of supernatural power to see the great persecutor who once visited from house to house to bind men and women and deliver them to prison, now going from house to house teaching and building up the little flock? To see such a man at work is to see God at work (*cf.* 4:13).

We may well be thankful for this classic interpretation of Christian ministry, and pray that more and more spiritual leaders in our own day may be found following this apostolic pattern.

[31] Phil. 2:12, 13.   [32] 1 Thes. 2:9; 1 Cor. 4:12.

Colossians 2:1-5
Apostolic concerns

F OR I want you to know how greatly I strive for you, and for those at Laodicea, and for all who have not seen my face, ²that their hearts may be encouraged as they are knit together in love, to have all the riches of assured understanding and the knowledge of God's mystery, of Christ, ³in whom are hid all the treasures of wisdom and knowledge. ⁴I say this in order that no one may delude you with beguiling speech. ⁵For though I am absent in body, yet I am with you in spirit, rejoicing to see your good order and the firmness of your faith in Christ.

In this section Paul continues to write of his ministry. But a division here is allowable. So far (1:24–29) Paul has explained the leading principles that guided him in his work with all the churches. This pattern of apostolic ministry was explained to the Colossians so that the church might have a standard of comparison against which to measure the style of the new teachers. But now the apostle addresses them more intimately. He begins to open his heart, and share with them his special hopes and concerns for their future.

A very few sentences like these suffice to show why Paul was so greatly loved. Modern caricatures of the apostle as forbidding or angular, unnecessarily cerebral and dogmatic, indifferent to women and ungracious to opponents, are a painful commentary on present-day ignorance of his letters. But it is a common experience that grotesque misunderstandings easily grow when we never meet people face to face, and have to depend on garbled or second-hand accounts of their attitudes.

From a careful reading of verses 1 and 5 it looks as if just such a

81

situation was in danger of arising in Colossae. The visitors were not without a capacity for disparagement, even malicious slander, if our understanding of Paul's swift defence of Epaphras is correct. The Colossians had never set eyes on the apostle nor heard him speak. In these circumstances it is not difficult to imagine that Paul's position could be misinterpreted, and mutual confidence damaged. All this would provide the perfect soil in which dissensions and divisions could grow.

Against this kind of background, Paul's words here leap to life. He tells the Colossians that he wants them to be aware of his personal interest in them, and the joy their stability gives him. He wants them to know that he is actively concerned for them (this seems to be the force of the word 'strive' which links with 'striving' in the previous verse, 1 : 29). And not just for them, but for the other Christian communities of the Lycus valley, especially the church at Laodicea, for similar perils threaten them all.

Three features stand out in what the apostle has to say to them.

1. Paul's special concern (verses 1-3)

The special concern of this paragraph is not immediately obvious. One commentator has preferred 'instructed' instead of 'knit together' (a reasonable preference since the verb can mean either) on the ground that unity is not an issue in this letter. But there is no practical issue more important in this paragraph or in the whole letter than that of unity! For Paul the most certain result of any acceptance of the new teaching will be a breach of fellowship in the church. Therefore his special concern for the Colossians is that they should continue to be united in love. He writes specifically to *encourage* (there is a flavour of affectionate admonition in this word) them to stick together.

The fine thing about this word of exhortation is the balance of it. The apostle recognizes that lasting unity depends upon *truth* as well as *love*. Christians have to be substantially of one mind as well as of one heart. That is why Paul wants all the Christians at Colossae to share that rich spiritual assurance that comes with the conviction that *all* the secret treasures of divine wisdom and insight are to be found in Christ. This seems to be the thrust of the remarkable words in verses 2 and 3. Once it is agreed among the brethren that there are no essential truths outside of Christ, and that therefore there can be no essential insights hidden from anyone who is now in Christ, it becomes possible to maintain mutual confidence and love among themselves.

But on the other hand, if there are those who claim an understanding of God beyond the ordinary 'man in Christ', and if certain believers claim to have found spiritual riches more than those which conversion and baptism into Christ have given them, then church unity will be seriously at risk.

Because disagreement here, at this central point, was seen by Paul to be so serious a matter, an interpreter could opt for the word 'instructed' rather than 'knit together', and claim that this binds the phrases together more coherently. Paul is then understood to be encouraging the brethren to instruct one another in love (a familiar Pauline thought),[1] so that they arrive at a common mind about Christ and his fullness, with all the stability that such agreement brings.

However, in view of the further use of 'knit together' in 2:19, the RSV translation is preferable.

2. Paul's special warning (verse 4)

If the unity of the church at Colossae was at risk, it is no surprise that Paul was deeply concerned. In his letters from prison the need for maintaining spiritual unity is repeatedly taught.[2] On this subject the apostle could offer quite definite and pertinent advice, and he is prepared to name names, as in Philippians 4:2.

Here in verse 4, some commentators have thought that Paul has his eye on one particular leader among the innovators of whom he has received reports. What is much more probable is that, from such reports, Paul has come to recognize a particular quality that appears to characterize this man and his helpers. There is a certain stamp about them. It is not so much what they say as how they say it that reveals them to Paul. For what is noticeable about them is that they are skilled in the arts of persuasion. Their speech proves in practice to be most *beguiling*.

There is of course nothing wrong in itself with the ability to persuade others. Paul himself was a highly skilful persuader from earliest days,[3] and he often urges other preachers to be the same.[4] But here the word is clearly given a negative meaning. There is a 'persuasiveness' that Paul fears.

[1] *E.g.* Eph. 4:15.   [2] *E.g.* Eph. 4:1ff.; Phil. 2:1ff.   [3] Acts 9:22.
[4] *E.g.* 2 Tim. 4:2.

The mark of these teachers, therefore, was that although their matter was false, their manner was such that people readily believed them. Their listeners were carried away by the eloquence and skill with which their case was presented. A more critical attitude towards what they said might have shown up the flaws in the argument. But people were in no mood for analysis when what they heard charmed and captivated them. The inevitable result followed; those who gave heed to these impressive and high-sounding speakers were *deluded* by them.

This powerful word, 'deluded', means simply that people were deceived and led astray from the right paths. The Greek word occurs in one other place in the New Testament, James 1:22, where it is used to refer to our capacity, even as Christians, to deceive ourselves. So listeners to the new teachers might also be self-deceived, wanting to believe what they heard. Possibly, too, some of the teachers themselves were not conscious deceivers of others, but self-deceived in their turn.

It was essential to listen to Paul's warning in his own day: it is even more essential to heed it in our day when the arts of persuasion, and the means by which they can be exercised, are so highly developed. There is a fresh responsibility laid on Christians to examine all teaching for the truthfulness of its content rather than the attractiveness of its packaging. There is a new call to be sceptical of exaggerated rhetoric, the tendentious anecdote, or the theatrical appeal, for nothing is so dangerous as feeble reasoning allied to fast talking.

There is also a responsibility on those who preach, to follow Paul in his renunciation of the smooth talk of the salesman, or the clever one-sided presentation of the propagandist. People's minds are far too easily influenced by these means today. It is not that there is evil in possessing gifts of persuasiveness so long as these gifts are harnessed to, and controlled by, sound thinking. But as our business is with truth, and with the God-given conviction that it brings,[5] all our methods of presentation should be as frank and truthful as we can make them.

3. Paul's special joy (verse 5)

This is a very happy verse. It gives the reader good hope that,

[5] 1 Cor. 2:1-5.

despite the dangers facing the Colossian church through 'false brethren', and all the many anxieties Paul felt, there was to be a happy ending to the whole affair nonetheless.

For the moment, at any rate, the situation as Paul saw it at Colossae was still cause for great joy. Though absent in body (the fetters saw to that, 4 : 18) he wants the Colossians to know that he is 'with them' in spirit, especially as their faith comes under fire.

We may allow ourselves this military metaphor since Paul makes use of similar army terminology when he describes the 'order' and 'firmness' of the church at Colossae. It is a natural use of language, perhaps used almost unconsciously, and suggests that despite the enticements of the false teachers, the Christians were standing firm with unbroken ranks. Their faith was still fixed, as we might say, foursquare on Christ alone.

By way of summarizing this gracious paragraph, it is worth underscoring the secret of unity that is revealed here. It is in the preaching of *Christ* that the churches find it possible to stand shoulder to shoulder, as modern campaigns of evangelistic enterprise have so often shown.

Obviously, if *less* than the Christ of 1 : 15–20 is believed among the churches, there will be no gospel to preach, no good news to offer. What is not quite so obvious, but is equally important, is that the united front so essential for convincing evangelism will be threatened when there are those in the churches teaching *more* than this Christ. We need to take very seriously Paul's claim that all our spiritual treasures are found in Christ alone if the powerful witness of a united band of Christian churches is to be exercised in the world.

Colossians 2:6-7
This way ahead

AS therefore you received Christ Jesus the Lord, so live in him,
⁷rooted and built up in him and established in the faith, just as
you were taught, abounding in thanksgiving.

These two verses summarize well the basic teaching of the
Colossian letter. Here is a concise description of what is required
of any church privileged to live under the watchful authority of
Paul. What is described is not only the way the young Christians
should be faithful to apostolic foundations (thus RSV links the
verses with the previous paragraph) but also how best they can
make good headway and yet be able to avoid the bogus spirituality
that threatened them (thus NEB links the verses with the following
section). Despite apparent simplicity, however, it is quite easy to
miss the significance of these important words. There is more
here than an exhortation to faithfulness and perseverance. We
shall need to approach them carefully if we are to discern what
was in Paul's mind as he wrote them.

We do not learn from error if we are content merely to expose
its follies. The new teaching had an immediate appeal just because
it spoke to a real need. Trying to see it at its best, and using the
warning passages in 2:8-23 in order to reconstruct its
characteristics, we can discover why it found a ready audience
among new believers.

It urged upon these young Christians the challenge of fullness
of spiritual life and experience. It called upon them to be satisfied
with nothing less than a life free from the stain and tyranny of sin.
It pointed the way to a zeal and devotion that put to shame all
complacence or half-heartedness. It spoke of the need to get out of

the shallows, and open the heart and mind to the deep things of God. It made much both of leaving the rudimentary stages of spirituality and of the possibilities of swift advance to a wider understanding.

We cannot possibly find fault with such hunger for God. Certainly we cannot satisfy that hunger by confining people to a limited circle of truth, repentance and faith, confession and absolution, conversion and the new birth, as though there were little more to Christianity than entering the kingdom. When someone begins with Christ he may reasonably be disappointed if we can point to no exciting signposts for the journey ahead. Can we do this, or is it a matter of patiently urging him to come back to the beginning every time he falters?

In these two verses the apostle gives authoritative guidance that helps to resolve these and similar questions. He holds two truths before us, insisting that they be held firmly in balance.

First he shows that 'receiving Christ' is not the end but the beginning of life; that foundations exist not for themselves, but to be built upon; and that what we first learnt opens to us a life of increasing knowledge. We shall need to take this to heart if we are going to be the overflowing Christians of God's purpose. At the same time Paul is equally plain in his teaching that all growth and progress in the Christian life must be entirely consistent with its beginnings. We shall need to take this to heart if we want a spirituality that is genuinely Christian, brings glory to God, and no disillusionment to us.

Paul gives the Colossians three guiding principles, each referring to a different aspect of Christian development, but similar in form.

1. As you received ... so live.
2. As you were rooted ... be built up.
3. As you were taught ... be established in truth.

These principles refer respectively to godly living, spiritual growth, and Christian understanding.

1. As you received ... so live

This is a summons to live out the Christian life in the sense of 1:10, a lifestyle worthy of the Lord. The old version, 'so *walk* ye in

87

him' has much to commend it, for to the reader of Paul this is familiar language for consistent Christian conduct.[1]

So Paul teaches that 'receiving Christ' is intended to lead on to a worthy walk in the paths of righteousness. This is the first thing for which the enthusiastic young believer should be full of zeal.[2] The balancing truth is that the 'walk' of the Christian should be wholly consistent with those spiritual beginnings when first he received Christ.

What does it mean to 'receive Christ'? If we are accustomed to present-day usage of this phrase, we are likely to have an inadequate understanding of it. When the earliest Christians 'received Christ' through Paul's ministry, what primarily they received from the apostle was an account of the gospel truths he had himself received from the risen Lord. Repeatedly Paul refers to this, as two examples from 1 Corinthians will show:

> I commend you because you remember me in everything and maintain the traditions even as I have delivered them to you.[3]

> Now I would remind you, brethren, in what terms I preached to you the gospel, which you received, in which you stand, by which you are saved, if you hold it fast—unless you believed in vain. For I delivered to you as of first importance what I also received, that Christ died for our sins in accordance with the scriptures, that he was buried, that he was raised on the third day...[4]

This oral tradition, most carefully treasured and guarded,[5] was to become the written tradition as we now have it in the New Testament.

What then the Corinthians and the Colossians 'received' was at least an account of Christ's death for their sins, and the well-attested fact of his rising on the third day. This is not to deny the necessity of the young Christians' heart submission to Christ. 'With the personal object here, the verb must include the further thought of "receive into the heart", so that the words become an appeal to the *experience* of the presence of Christ, which was the beginning of new spiritual life for the Colossians.'[6]

---

[1] *E.g.* Eph. 5:2, 8, 15.   [2] *Cf.* Tit. 2:14.   [3] 1 Cor. 11:2.
[4] 1 Cor. 15:1-3.   [5] 1 Tim. 6:20; 2 Tim. 1:12-14.
[6] Beare, p. 188: his italics. *Cf.* Moule, p. 89.

The application of this to evangelism is obviously important if we are to avoid spurious commitments to Christ and the phenomenon of a large number of people dropping out of the Christian race almost before they have begun. To pray with a casual contact to 'receive Christ' may show more zeal than wisdom if the basic and essential traditions of the Christian story and message have not been made clear and assimilated. Jesus has to be 'learned' in order to be 'received'.[7]

Part of this understanding that we must ask of an enquirer is a recognition of Christ as Lord. Again our tendency is to speak of receiving Christ as Saviour rather than as Lord. Worse still, we even catch ourselves half hiding the authoritative demands of the Lord in our eagerness to commend the attractive offers of the Saviour. When this happens, the only thing to be hidden is our heads in shame! For this way of talking turns the gospel upside down. Jesus can be our Saviour only because he is Lord. He must have unquestioned authority over the powers of evil before he can possibly deliver us from them.

This, for example, is why Mark's Gospel begins the story of Jesus as the appearance of an Authority who could not be denied. All other authorities, of whatever kind (the will of man, ancient traditions of truth, demons, disease, the powers of nature, and even the powers of death) must yield to him.[8]

To 'receive Christ Jesus the Lord', then, is to recognize as truth the marvellous news that, in Christ, the Lord who has power to redeem the world from error and misery has come. More than that, the words necessarily imply the appropriate submission to that Lord for personal deliverance. This means that 'life in the Spirit' is recognizable, according to Paul, by some genuine acknowledgment of Christ's lordship.[9] True conversion must imply a recognition of Christ's right to be my Saviour (after all, most of us do not very much want to be saved from all our sins, only from their penalty).

We are now in a better position to understand what Paul's first summons to the Colossians means. True conversion implies the right of Christ to rule, and therefore to determine the shape and character of what in his eyes is worthy and consistent living. His pleasure is first to be consulted. The Christian therefore comes to

---

[7] 1:7; cf. Eph. 4:20, 21.
[8] Mk. 1:18, 22, 27, 34; 2:10, 14, 28; 4:41; 5:42.   [9] 1 Cor. 12:3.

any and every situation willingly recognizing that the writ of Christ's authority runs there.

The challenge is to 'make Christ Lord' in all our human affairs; yet this is not an altogether happy phrase, since now that the Colossians are 'in Christ' he *is* their Lord (notwithstanding their often rebellious hearts) with full intent to 'make them' his obedient servants![10] The experience of every Christian tallies with this. The chastenings and corrections we receive are all evidence that Christ is exercising his lordship.

One illustration may be enough to show that to live in Christ as Lord, acknowledging his authority in all things, could set perplexing problems. This concerns the first-century slave as portrayed in 3:22ff. How is he to order his life after conversion to Christ? All his days he has known but one overriding 'authority', his master, who in law owns him body and soul, and orders all his affairs. But now, in Christ, the slave knows a new Lord who claims full authority over him and his future. What can this mean in practice? Should the Christian slave refuse to acknowledge the claims of the human authority under which he has hitherto lived, and sign his own death warrant for Christ's sake? Or should he revolt (which in practice means running away) as the only way of expressing his new determination to obey God rather than man? Here are questions fit for a Solomon. Yet 1:9 and 10 have suggested that this is just the sort of wisdom the believing slave can call upon! We must wait until a study of 3:22ff. for an answer.

2. As you were rooted ... be built up

This is a summons to grow in Christ. It immediately reminds us that the *building up* of young Christians was a major concern of the apostle's. This may be partly hidden by the slightly old-fashioned 'edify' and 'edification' of the older translations.

Yet the idea of building adequately and firmly on the foundation of Christ is a vivid and important one in the New Testament.[11] We are to make the building up of one another our chief concern. For Paul, many questions can be decided by the simple rule, 'Let all things be done for edification.'[12]

So there is no doubt that Paul has little patience with a constant

[10] *Cf.* Mk. 1:17.
[11] *E.g.* Rom. 15:2; 1 Cor. 14 (*passim*); Eph. 4:12, 16, 29; 1 Thes. 5:11.
[12] 1 Cor. 14:26.

laying again of foundations, spoken of in Hebrews 6:1. He calls for the Christian, once 'rooted in Christ' (a perfect participle), to 'be built up in Christ' (a present participle).

Even the metaphor used suggests that conversion is only a beginning. (Incidentally Paul may not be mixing his metaphors here, since the word 'rooted' was also used in his day for sinking the foundations of buildings:[13] but in any case metaphorical language in common use soon tends to lose its distinctive figurative meaning). We hardly bury a seed, or bulb, in the soil hoping to see the last of it. And the mark of gospel seed has always been vigorous growth (1:6).

This time the balancing truth is that, as the *rooting* was 'in Christ', so the *growing* must also be 'in him'. According to Paul we cannot find (and therefore should not seek) a different element in which to grow than that in which we were planted.

We are called to take this much more seriously than we do. To be 'in Christ' is to occupy the richest position that can be ours this side of heaven. Of course there is infinite scope to explore the fullness of Christ, otherwise the believer would not be exhorted to seek the Christ who has already found him (3:1). But we ought to think very carefully before claiming that no growth to full maturity for the young convert is likely, or even possible, unless he is transplanted into some richer soil. For example, we must ask our catholic friend whether or not he believes that full salvation and security can belong only to those who enjoy the sacramental life of his church under the guidance and authority of the Roman See. Similarly we must ask our pentecostal friend how he can justify the claim that while baptism into Christ gives life, a distinct baptism in the Spirit is necessary for full vigour and fruitfulness of spiritual experience.

If it is in Christ, and in Christ alone, that all treasures are to be found, are such friends asking us to believe that this Christ cannot be fully enjoyed and known except in circles where their own peculiar (in the sense of special) doctrines are accepted and taught? History knows no church, however rich in achievements, no group of Christians, however blessed, who can hold Christ within their own borders, and therefore demand submission to their authority or teaching as the price of full incorporation into the deep things of God.

[13]Beare, p. 188.

This, emphatically, is not to deny that the fullness of Christ the Head can be ours only within his body (2:19). But it is to assert the freedom of the individual Christian from those spiritual tyrannies that must develop if the keys of the kingdom are held by frail human hands.

3. As you were taught ... be established in truth

This is a summons to deeper Christian understanding. It is the third example Paul gives of the urgent need to grow up to our full stature, this time in knowledge. To be *established in the faith* is to be consolidated in the truth (faith here is not the believer's trust but the apostle's teaching).

As usual with Paul there is this great stress on the importance of teaching. Without the full truth, and a mature understanding of it, there cannot be a satisfying Christianity or a stable church. So, according to Paul, a hallmark of the Spirit's work is an unquenchable thirst to learn.

But once more there is a balancing caution here that is quite unmistakeable. The new learning must be consistent with the old. The Christian who grows in knowledge can claim fuller enlightenment only in so far as he remains loyal to the saving gospel truths that first he was taught, and which led him to Christ.

This has something uncomfortably trenchant to say to Christian leaders. Did not many owe their first knowledge of Christ to evangelical truth? Yet how many now say that they have 'grown out' of such simplicities. But to grow beyond the saving truths as we were faithfully taught them is not to grow up in a way that can please God or profit the church. Such fancied superiority in knowledge calls for honest self-examination to see if true loyalty to Christ remains.

This is not a plea for obscurantism, or the vain repetition of shibboleths. It is not to ask that youthful immaturities of expression should fail to get the decent burial they deserve. Most surely it is not a call to deaden the spirits and harden the hearts of congregations like an old gospel preacher, often recalled, of whom it was said, 'Ten thousand thousand were his texts, but all his sermons one.'

But it is a call to today's Timothys, who have growing responsibilities crowding in upon them, not to be 'ashamed of testifying to our Lord, nor of (Paul) his prisoner, but share in suffering for the gospel in the power of God.'[14] Notice that loyalty to Christ's gospel involved Timothy in loyalty to Paul, the one whose teaching brought him to faith in Christ.

The threefold summons of this section then shows that Paul is no friend to complacency. He calls his readers to a wholly consistent way of life, to fullness of spiritual stature, and to comprehensiveness of knowledge. But let it be true growth which is always a harmonious development of the saving gospel of Christ.

Finally he adds a most telling phrase. Those who follow his call are to be *overflowing with thanksgiving*.

Is this the jargon of the new teachers again? Did they speak of the 'overflowing life', or (following the AV) the 'abundant life'? It seems very likely. Well, Paul believes in fullness too. He sees faithful Christians as 'overflowing', and the cup that runs over is, beyond controversy, full! But of what does this overflow consist?

It is 'evermore thanks, the exchequer of the poor'.[15] This may well reveal the contrast in outlook between Paul and the new teachers. The visitors presumably made much of the spiritual wealth that would belong to those who accepted what they said. But does not experience discover many perils along this path—perils of spiritual conceit and boastfulness, as Paul found at Corinth,[16] and now sees with alarm in the new teachers at Colossae (2:18)? Those who lay down conditions for occupying higher ground often leave the ground of 'grace'. (And people have left that ground whenever they thank God that they are not as others.)[17] The language of lofty spiritual claims is terribly close to the language of cant.

To be bursting with thankfulness is a true witness of the Spirit within us. For the voice of thanksgiving speaks without ceasing of the goodness of God. It claims nothing. It sees no merit in man's receiving but only in God's giving. It marvels at his mercy. It is the language of joy just because it need look no longer to its own resources. It is an expression of dependence on another. It is the speech of the Psalmist and is the natural tongue of the apostles. It is also heard on the lips of the 'weakest Christian on his knees'.

Here is a fine test by which we may test the authentic quality of our spiritual growth. To be 'filled with gratitude' is to be 'filled

[14] 2 Tim. 1:8.　　[15] W. Shakespeare, *Richard II*, II. iii. 65.
[16] 2 Cor. 10-12.　　[17] Lk. 18:9-14.

with the Spirit of Christ'. The Christian rejoicing in this blessing of a thankful heart will have his eyes fixed upon the right person and the right place, Christ at God's right hand. He cannot be taken up with himself without being immediately reminded that everything he possesses is the gift of God. The only thing which he can claim to be filled with, which comes from himself, and which he can offer to God, is gratitude.

But that is not to deny that we are all tempted, from time to time, to play the Pharisee again.

Colossians 2:8-15

No return to slavery

*S*EE *to it that no one makes a prey of you by philosophy and empty deceit, according to human tradition, according to the elemental spirits of the universe, and not according to Christ.* [9]*For in him the whole fullness of deity dwells bodily,* [10]*and you have come to fullness of life in him, who is the head of all rule and authority.* [11]*In him also you were circumcised with a circumcision made. without hands, by putting off the body of flesh in the circumcision of Christ;* [12]*and you were buried with him in baptism, in which you were also raised with him through faith in the working of God, who raised him from the dead.* [13]*And you, who were dead in trespasses and the uncircumcision of your flesh, God made alive together with him, having forgiven us all our trespasses,* [14]*having cancelled the bond which stood against us with its legal demands; this he set aside, nailing it to the cross.* [15]*He disarmed the principalities and powers and made a public example of them, triumphing over them in him.*

The section from verse 8 to verse 19 consists of three warnings. Already we know that Paul recognized the need for a ministry of warning in the churches to complement the more positive teaching ministry (1:28). He himself was never frightened to sound an alarm, though no doubt this sometimes led to his being dubbed a tiresome and intolerant trouble-maker.[1] So his cautionary 'beware' becomes familiar in the AV and is made more vivid through modern translations.[2] Here he tells the Colossians

[1] *Cf.* Elijah, 1 Ki. 18:17.
[2] *E.g.* 'Take care' (1 Cor. 8:9 RSV); 'Watch out' (Phil. 3:2 LB and GNB); 'Look out' (Phil. 3:2 RSV).

to be on their guard against the activities of the visitors. The three ways in which he raises the alarm are forceful and expressive.

1. Don't let anyone kidnap you! (verse 8).
2. Don't let anyone condemn you! (verse 16).
3. Don't let anyone disqualify you! (verse 18).

We shall look at the second and third warnings in the next two chapters. Here, we deal with the warning in verses 8ff.: 'Don't let anyone kidnap you!'

Someone is out to capture the Colossians' allegiance. But it is worse than that. The unusual word used here speaks of the slave-raider carrying off his victim, body and soul. These plausible teachers may say that they come to bring Christians new liberties but, says Paul in effect, don't go near them if you value your spiritual freedom. It is fortunate that Paul does not mince his words, for here proselytism is called by its right name.

Verse 8 may be analysed in this way:

Visitors' claim	To teach the full knowledge of God.
Paul's verdict	Their claim is false.
Visitors' claim	Their credentials are primitive tradition and spiritual authority.
Paul's verdict	Their credentials are false.

The word *philosophy* has no reference to the work of Greek philosophy which neither the visitors, nor Paul, were extolling or disparaging. It was commonplace for contemporary sects and cults to offer a deep *knowledge* of divine mysteries, and the visitors must have been making some more or less pretentious claims along these lines. Either they offered to Christians in particular the fullest possible experience of spiritual enlightenment, or they saw in their teaching the way of mature intelligence which would satisfy those who had 'outgrown' the simplicities of apostolic teaching. But in whatever way it was put, the appeal of the new teachers owed more to human than divine wisdom.[3]

Paul's sharp verdict is that this much-acclaimed 'teaching' is empty of content. Their claims are misleading and untrue. Despite convincing testimony to the contrary, the Emperor is

[3] *Cf.* 1 Cor. 1:18–25.

wearing no clothes. As the apostle wrote on a similar occasion, 'Let no one deceive you with *empty* words.'[4]

Inevitably, with such high-sounding talk, the visitors would be challenged to produce their credentials. Since, in our human affairs, traditions, with their claim to antiquity, legitimize many things that might otherwise be questioned, it seems likely that the challenge was met by an appeal to traditional authority. So the visitors would claim that there was nothing new in their religious philosophy. Perhaps there were even great names to which they could appeal.

What the new teachers looked for to authenticate their views will be recognizable by any negotiator in church unity schemes. The older churches in particular lay stress on sacred traditions handed down by the pious through the generations from apostolic times, all under the guidance of the Spirit.

So Paul's tradition[5] is challenged by another tradition claiming to co-exist with it. Yet the apostle can dare to settle the matter by calling other traditions merely *human*, while his apostleship (and therefore his message) is 'not from men nor through man, but through Jesus Christ and God the Father.'[6] The issue that arises when 'the traditions of men' clash with 'the word of God' has been decided by our Lord once and for all.[7] There is no way of healing disunity in the churches if we shuffle or evade that decision.

Further, the visitors laid claim to a high spiritual authority for their teaching because of their familiarity with the 'elements of the universe'. An alternative rendering of these words is the 'elementary ideas belonging to this world' (NEB margin), and some commentators on Colossians[8] have argued powerfully for this in preference to the RSV. At least one rather characteristic Pauline irony would follow this reading. The teaching which laid such claims to be 'advanced', Paul would dismiss as rudimentary, or as we should say, just ABC stuff ('elements', Gk. *stoicheia*, meaning the letters of the alphabet as written in order).

But the position taken here is that the RSV is to be preferred, especially in view of verse 10b. We will not attempt to grasp the many notions circulating in the world of Paul's day concerning the heavenly powers which ruled human fate. Whatever mumbo-jumbo about astrological forces and cosmic powers was common

---

[4]Eph. 5:6.   [5]See comments on 2:6, pp. 106ff.   [6]Gal. 1:1.
[7]Mk. 7:1–13.   [8]Moule, pp. 90f.

in the Lycus valley, we shall assume that the visiting teachers were not another set of superstitious pagans. But nevertheless they were far too occupied with the demonic powers that undoubtedly do exist. They claimed an awareness of these principalities, and a power over them, that easily gave authority to their ministry, especially among the gullible.

Yet Paul rejects these credentials. They are not 'according to Christ'. For it is *in him* that Christians exclusively find the conqueror of these evil powers that seek to tyrannize the world. Christ dealt them a decisive blow at his cross, so that wherever that victory is proclaimed, their overthrow is certain. The claim of the visitors to possess a special spiritual authority over demonic forces is superfluous. They can add nothing to Christ's victory. Therefore they have nothing substantial to offer those who are in Christ.

In verse 8 Paul rejects the new teachers as imposters and their claims as unwarrantable. These claims, remember, were to bring to the church a new spiritual 'freedom', through the gift to the Christians of a new spiritual 'fullness'.

Of course Paul is not content simply to label the new teaching as harmful and misleading; the whole situation gives him an opportunity, not to be missed, to expound the treasures that already belong to those in Christ. Once the Colossians understand their position of privilege in Christ, it is inconceivable that they will want to look elsewhere than to Christ for spiritual satisfaction. Paul's steady aim with all young converts was that they should have such adequate instruction that they will not 'remain as children at the mercy of every chance wind of teaching and the jockeying of men who are expert in the crafty presentation of lies'.[9]

So, in verses 9–15, Paul gives to the church at Colossae (and therefore to the universal church) an almost uniquely valuable summary of what it means to be 'in Christ'.

This paragraph is so concentrated (Paul's ability to condense is nowhere more in evidence than in Colossians, to the frequent embarrassment of commentators) that this study is arranged in three sub-sections. In this way it will be easier to appreciate the particular details, as well as the direction and cumulative force of the whole section, just as no careful reader can miss what

[9]Eph. 4:14JBP.

Lohse has called the 'motif' of these verses in the repeated use of the phrases 'in him' and 'with him', a characteristic already noted.

1. Verses 9 and 10   Fullness in Christ
2. Verses 11 and 12   Fellowship with Christ
3. Verses 13–15   Freedom through Christ

As we study these three sections, we shall discover two themes which thread their way through the whole paragraph, sometimes interwoven, sometimes separate.

(i) United with Christ, believers now share in *all* that he has won.

(ii) In Christ, believers now have all that can be theirs *in this world*.

1. Fullness in Christ (verses 9–10)

No words can better describe the place Christ has in the purpose of God for man's salvation.

First, *in him*, all that deity means is now dwelling! Think for a moment of what deity does mean to the Christian mind. It means the 'Creator, who is blessed for ever'. It means the great 'I am'. It means the 'only Sovereign, the King of kings and Lord of lords, who alone has immortality'.[10]

With such titles in mind, consider again the scope of the words, 'the whole fullness of deity'. And then recognize, surely with awe, that this fullness of Godhead dwells in Christ.

The concept of 'dwelling' with reference to God in Christ always refers to the divine condescension in coming to us to be accessible to us, that is, to be 'At Home' to us. Since the Christ of Colossians is now ascended and reigning at God's right hand, this throne of grace is now the place where God is accessible to us.

What then is the position of privilege for all Christ's people, at Colossae as in all the world? Paul gives the splendid answer: *'You have come to fullness of life in him.'* Note each vital phrase.

You have come. Yes, with Paul, verb tenses can be remarkably illuminating. Such fullness is not for future attainment, since already the Colossians *have come* to it.

Fullness of life. The emphasis on 'fullness' in these two verses

---

[10] Rom. 1:25; Ex. 3:13–15; 1 Tim. 6:15.

may well mean that this was the very terminology of the visitors.[11]

In him! This is the sole place of full divine blessing, for it is here alone that God has fully given himself to us.

So Paul will not have 'fullness' taken away from Christ, or from his people. This means that in Paul's teaching, to 'receive Christ' is to be 'filled'. Forgiveness and redemption are precisely the gift of fullness. Has someone come to Christ for salvation? Then he has found in the Lord fullness of life. This is the apostolic language.

Not only so, but the believer already shares Christ's victory, for is not Christ now *head of all rule and authority* (verse 10)? Of this supreme authority over all spiritual powers, the church is the beneficiary, enjoying in Christ perfect freedom from all his enemies. Christians are freed from the dominion of darkness, and need fear these demonic powers no more.

Already our two themes stand revealed. With regard to the fullness of God's presence with us on earth, in Christ *we have all that can be ours* this side of heaven. With regard to heaven's victory over powers and principalities, *we share with Christ all that he has won.*

2. Fellowship with Christ (verses 11–12)

It is probable that the visitors made much of a deeper union with God as a spiritual prize for those who accepted their teaching. At any rate, in this section Paul seems anxious to show the young convert just what it means to him to have union and fellowship already with the Christ who died and rose again. Once more Paul chooses the tenses of his verbs with great care. Is it that the visitors offered a deeper experience of dying and rising with Christ leading to a new release from the clinging power of sin? But writes Paul, in your conversion/baptism, you *were* 'circumcised', you *were* 'buried' with Christ, you *were* 'raised' with him. All this lies in the past. What Christ then did, the Christian now shares with him. It has already happened as far as they are concerned. But what does this mean?

a. You were circumcised (verse 11)
We should not look to the Galatian church for a parallel here. It is

[11] Lohse, p. 100.

unlikely that this was an attempt to 'compel the Gentiles to live like Jews'.[12] As Beare points out, there is no evidence of Jewish nationalism at Colossae.[13] It is more satisfactory to see submission to circumcision as an act of dedication and consecration (as in the history of the Mau Mau in Kenya), urged on the Colossians by the new teachers. It stood for a second initiation subsequent to baptism. By this the believer would enter his full inheritance.

In view of Paul's language it is not particularly difficult to guess the nature of the new teaching on this point. The outward act would symbolize a stripping off of the 'body of flesh', so that the new initiate could expect to step forward to an experience of freedom from the dragging downward pull of the 'flesh' and all its works.[14]

In the history of the church, some earnest seekers after holiness have seen even the body itself as a drastic hindrance to a clearer vision of God. But here the 'body of flesh' means not our human body of flesh and blood, but what Paul calls 'the flesh', that permanent propensity for evil that continues within us after conversion/baptism. While I am in the body, the 'flesh' is in me, hence the inevitable link between the two. The 'flesh' will be part of my experience until death. Nevertheless the Christian faith never sees the body itself, or the materials of which it is made up, as anything but good. This body therefore cannot hamper me in my search for God and goodness (as dualism teaches). Yet all Christians sadly admit that the 'flesh' remains a discouraging hindrance to their efforts to live consistently.

Every true disciple of Christ, then, grieves over his own carnality (fleshliness). 'The law is spiritual; but I am carnal',[15] laments Paul, for though he loved the law he could, even as a Christian, never fully attain it. Paul well knew how the young Christians at Colossae would be longing for freedom from the pull of the 'flesh'. He also knows how open this will make them to false promises of just such a freedom from the 'flesh' that may be offered to them. In this new work of God was offered a purification from 'the body of flesh'; in short, the new teachers may well have been offering what has often been called 'the clean heart'.

Now Paul's striking answer is that the Colossians already

---

[12] Gal. 2:14.   [13] Beare, p. 196.   [14] Gal. 5:19-21.
[15] Rom. 7:14. It is often the mark of fanaticism to reverse the order of this sentence.

possess the only purification of which Christ is the source. This 'circumcision without hands' (*i.e.* an inward experience) is theirs already in Christ. The 'circumcision of Christ' is the purification he gives.[16]

This purification is none other than the forgiveness of sins, the great blessing of Christian initiation, evidently disparaged by the visitors, but celebrated by Paul throughout this letter.

In this supreme benefit of redemption Christians have all that can be theirs of purification in this life. To be cleansed from all unrighteousness, that is their joy: to be without sin is not now their privilege. In this present life, the 'flesh' remains to be mortified (3:5).

b. You were buried, verse 12a

Being baptized into Christ means sharing the benefits of his death as well as his resurrection. This is familiar teaching.[17] Here Paul touches very briefly on the Christian's union with Christ in his death, and he does so in terms of 'burial' with Christ. In the earliest statements of Christian belief, the burial of Christ is significantly emphasized.[18] It remains the proof that Jesus was truly dead before the resurrection.

Here then the Christians are told they are sharers in Christ's burial, because they *were* buried with him. In truth therefore they can claim that already they have died with Christ. But this, surely, in a very different sense from that often used since, when the claim is made that the root of sin itself can somehow be killed off, and thus put right out of God's sight altogether as a discarded corpse. Such a hope that, by the power of God, sin in the believer can be 'dead and buried' unhappily continues to reappear among Christians.

But there is no idea in Paul's teaching in this letter that the evil principle within man can be rooted out once and for all or even effectively neutralized. That is not the significance of the famous statement about the person who has 'put off the old nature with its practices' (3:9). What has happened is that the believer shared with Christ in his death. The judgment of God fell upon Christ, and, in him, those who are his died too. The old unregenerate man

---

[16] Some commentators understand 'the circumcision of Christ' to refer to the cross. Neil, p. 43; Moule, pp. 94f.

[17] Rom. 6:3, 4.

[18] *E.g.* 1 Cor. 15:4; *cf.* 'dead, and buried' in the Apostles' Creed.

has been judged, and condemned, and finally sentenced. Yet in Christ, he is raised to a new life. But for this new man there can be no further condemnation, since the inexorable link between sin and death has been broken.[19] For him therefore, death, not as a biological fact, *but as the wages of sin*, is over.

Death is an enemy because it separates man from all he knows and loves. It is the ultimate enemy because it separates men as sinners from God. Sharing in Christ's death does not exempt Christians from the death of this mortal body, but it does deliver them here and now from any liability to receive the wages of sin. That death Christ has died, and all who are in Christ share in the benefits of that finished work of atonement. Nothing can *now* separate the believer from the love of God in Christ.

There would be little gospel in all this if the Christian were actually 'freed from the flesh' in Christ, rather than from its condemnation. There could then be no surprise if such a person were acceptable in God's sight. But it is just because, though baptized and believing, the Christian is not yet free from sin's corruption,[20] that, according to Paul's gospel, grace triumphs still.

Once more Paul is teaching the Christians at Colossae that they already have, in Christ, *all that can be theirs* in this life. Sin remains, but separation from God has gone. Sadly, they are still carnal, yet not condemned. So they may draw near to God with thankfulness, knowing that his is still a throne of grace.

c. You were raised, verse 12b
By the power of God, Christ was raised from the dead. In this mighty act the Christians share. At conversion, they *were* raised with Christ.

There is no reference here to a future resurrection. Paul is speaking of present experience. This experience is the new life in the Spirit. It is this 'risen life', celebrated in 3 : 1, which became the present possession of the Colossians when they were raised with Christ through faith in the power of God. And it is this additional phrase about their faith that is significant here. It explains how what Christ did has become of benefit to them. Some commentators have noted that this sentence protects the sacrament of baptism from any idea that it is efficacious without faith in God, but it is doubtful if this is in Paul's mind here. It is

---

[19] Rom. 8 : 1.   [20] 1 Jn. 1 : 8.

more probable that his watchful eye is, as ever, on the emphases of the new teachers. If it is true that they were urging the young Christians to exercise faith in God for a fuller experience of divine power, these words of Paul could hardly have been more aptly chosen. What the apostle shows is that it was their initial faith in God that led the Colossians to experience God's mighty power when he raised them to newness of life. In this way the Christian has *already* shared with Christ in his resurrection. The implication of this is important. Paul is teaching the Christians to recognize the greatest manifestation of divine power (the power that raised Christ from the grave) in that sovereign act of mercy whereby sinful people are brought to reconciliation, forgiveness, and the new birth. The immensity of that change from darkness to light is constantly spoken of in this letter (1:13, 21, 22; 2:13; 3:10, 12). Nothing that God does for a Christian after conversion is comparable to this. It is true that one day the Christian will share still more of the resurrection power of God when he is 'raised incorruptible' on the last day. But that is not an experience in this life, which is Paul's interest here. It is the apostle's special concern, once more, to show the Colossians that in Christ they have already received all that they can receive from their share in his death and resurrection *in this life*. One day, divine power will lift them out of this realm of tears and tribulation to enjoy life beyond death. What they have now is life before death, the new life of the Spirit, the life of faith, above all the life of union and fellowship with the ascended Christ. How can anyone teach them that by faith in God, they may enjoy some greater blessing than that?[21]

3. Freedom through Christ (verses 13-15)

This third section continues the same themes. Yet it has a distinctive note in that God himself becomes the subject of the sentences:[22] it is as though Paul wishes to show them God himself

[21] An Ephesian fanaticism was later to claim that full and complete resurrection was also a present blessing of the gospel (2 Tim. 2:18). In that case, if the Christian should die, presumably faith must claim him back from the dead.

[22] Whether Christ has returned as the subject of the sentence by verse 15 is a matter of debate. No certain answer can be given, for Paul has not made it clear. The ease with which 'God' and 'Christ' are by now used by him interchangeably is of obvious significance, though in view of 1:15ff. it is no great surprise.

in action. Such 'divine activity' is not something that can follow only an acceptance of the new teaching and its emphases. Once again it seems that Paul is countering any suggestion that God can do for people anything greater than he has already done for them in Christ. And he does this, characteristically, by freshly describing for the Colossians the sheer immensity of what God has already done for them through the death of Christ. Truly he has brought them from death to life and from slavery to freedom!

Verse 13 is now a recognizable hallmark of Paul's style.[23] Briefly the grim situation before conversion is outlined. They had been open transgressors and godless heathen. As such they were 'dead' in God's sight: separated from God himself they were separate too from God's own people, those of the circumcision. Only 'life from the dead' could meet their need; not religion, philosophy, nor even moral exertion, supposing they had the heart for it. This great change came about through God's activity in and through Christ. Raised with Christ, all that was his was now theirs.[24]

Their conversion then was a great act of God, an act of incomparable power which could be described adequately only by the language of death and resurrection. Now in this creative act of God, the Colossians had been born free! To demonstrate this Paul uses some most dramatic terms to explain how, at the cross of Christ, the authority of sin and evil had been overthrown. And in doing this he gives to the church a magnificent summary of the gospel of Christ. We shall appreciate this summary the better for three preliminary observations.

(i) *The blessings of the gospel are twofold.* Baptism into Christ (that is, the work of the Spirit which unites us to Christ, signified and sealed but not automatically conveyed by water baptism) brings with it not only the forgiveness of all our sins (verse 14) but also deliverance from all the powers of evil (verse 15). We cannot speak of the enjoyment of one of these privileges without the other. This essential link is characteristic of Colossians, as a careful study of 1:13-14 and 2:9-10, will show. These two gifts, inseparable from Christ, are inseparable from one another. In giving us Christ, it is not possible even for God to give the first and withhold the second. For apostolic Christianity,

---

[23] *Cf.* 1:21 as well as a parallel passage in Eph. 2:1.
[24] Eph. 2:4-10 is the best expansion of verse 13.

where there is forgiveness of sins there is also freedom from the powers of evil. Indeed what a strange gift it otherwise would be, to have the past forgiven with no assurance of the future—to be free from Satan's accusations now that that old serpent has been thrown down,[25] yet not to be free from other aspects of his power! Such would be a poor salvation, and not the full and complete victory of Christ that Paul preached. In any case we ought not to make so stark a distinction between sin's penalty and its power as has often been done. Sin, in Paul's thinking, is always a sovereign power:[26] to be forgiven is to be free from the wages of sin which is death, so that in forgiveness itself the power of sin has been manifestly broken. There is no forgiveness in New Testament theology which is not at the same time life from the dead (*e.g.* Jn. 5:24; Acts 2:38).

(ii) *The blessings of the gospel were perfectly won for us at the cross of Christ.* It is Paul's clearest intention in verses 14 and 15 to show the decisive finality of the cross in winning for his people perfect freedom from the condemnation and power of sin. The demands of the law were nailed *to the cross* and thereby *cancelled.* The evil principalities were disarmed and overthrown at *the cross.*

A good commentary on verse 14 is Hebrews 10:11–18,[27] the heart of which is the statement, 'Where there is forgiveness ... there is no longer any offering for sin' (verse 18). The church cannot find in such emphatic language any commission to renew, replenish, or re-enact the once-for-all offering of the body of Jesus Christ. Together with Colossians 2:13, 14 it explains why any understanding of the Mass as an offering of Christ remains as much an offence as ever to Christians who wish to be true to biblical foundations.

But we must also insist, if we would be biblical, that our liberation from the 'principalities and powers' was as definitely and decisively accomplished at the cross of Christ as our forgiveness. Just as the Spirit of God teaches the church to look only to Christ's cross as the place where sin's claims are cancelled, so he teaches the church to look only to Christ's cross as the place where deliverance was won. It would be as much a misunderstanding to look to the Holy Spirit (leave alone any human being)

---

[25] Rev. 12:9f.   [26] *E.g.* Rom. 5:21.

[27] There seem to be many close affinities between the two letters, as noticed already.

as the winner of our deliverance as it would be to look to him rather than to Christ as the winner of our reconciliation. The work of the Spirit is, as ever, to declare to us what is inalienably Christ's that he (Christ) and he alone, may be glorified.[28] By illuminating our minds, by softening our hard hearts, by guiding and strengthening our wills, the Spirit leads us into an increasing experience of the deliverance that Christ won for us.

(iii) *The blessings of the gospel are openly made known to all believers.* We are aroused by the hammer blows of verse 14: our attention is caught and held by the dishevelled captives in Christ's triumphal procession described in verse 15. It is obviously no part of God's plan that there should be any secret about either of these achievements. But in the emphases of the new teaching we have already noticed an apparent pride in speaking of 'mysteries' revealed only to a few privileged souls. It is hard to avoid the impression that Paul is alluding to this tendency to deal in spiritual 'secrets'. (Was the danger in Colossae a form of the spiritual infantilism so often noted by the apostle in his letters to Corinth?[29]) At any rate it is clearly Paul's conviction that the cross of Christ in and of itself gives the clearest and most complete understanding to the Christian of the fullness that is in the gospel. Understand the cross, and it is impossible to miss what God has done for us. How then did Paul preach Christ crucified? In verses 14 and 15 we possess a particularly fine example of the 'word of the cross' which proves itself in every generation to be the power of God for salvation.

a. The bond was cancelled (verse 14)
This '*bond*', or 'certificate of indebtedness' (Lohse) is to be understood as a promissory note. It acknowledges that we are bound to keep God's laws and satisfy his rightful demands. For the Jew this was unarguable. Yet in fact all men and women show this sense of obligation through the many fresh resolutions, vows and promises they make, if only to themselves, to satisfy their consciences.[30] Our plight is fully brought home to us only when in all seriousness we attempt, like the young Martin Luther, to square our accounts with God. Then, at last, our danger as well as our incapacity become apparent. We cannot pay the debt we owe.

---

[28] Jn. 16:14.   [29] *E.g.* 1 Cor. 3:1; 13:11; 14:20.
[30] *Cf.* Rom. 2:14-16.

The bond stands *against us*. It makes its *legal*, and inescapable, *demands*. But Christ has *cancelled the bond*; the word here is more familiar to Bible students when translated 'blotted out' or 'wiped away'.[31] Whether or not there was a wax surface on many ancient bonds, this cancellation implies the total obliteration of any mark, 'jot or tittle', that remains against us. The Bible preachers and writers use many metaphors to bring home to forgiven sinners that when God forgives, no stain on the soul remains.[32] Here, however, it is not so much the stain that is removed but the legal demands that are met, a familiar element in Paul's teaching.[33] Hence we can go free without a stain on our record, released from any dread sentence of interminable years in which to pay.

b. The bond was set aside (verse 14)

'Set aside' is more familiarly rendered as 'taken away'. As such it is prominent in the New Testament preaching of the cross.[34] Now God has taken away the bond, setting aside its claims *on us*, by nailing it to Christ's cross. It has proved impossible to discover any ancient practice where a nail was driven through a bond in order to cancel it. An attractive idea is to imagine that Paul was thinking of the Roman *titulus* such as Pilate wrote and put on the cross, the remarkable story of which is recorded in John 19:19–22. To place a written accusation above every condemned criminal meant at least that a man's crimes, placarded for everyone to see and read, might serve as a justification for his punishment as well as a warning to others. In our Lord's case the accusation was a mockery, as Pilate well knew. Yet, according to the apostolic preaching, there was an accusation nailed there in God's purposes, an accusation *against us* yet borne by Christ. 'Christ redeemed us from the curse of the law, having become a curse for us—for it is written, "Cursed be every one who hangs on a tree."' The dreadful words of Galatians 3:13 make the clearest possible comment on 2:14. The curse and condemnation of a broken law belonged to the Colossians before their conversion. It has now been set aside, not in the sense of being overlooked and ignored, but because in Christ it has already been exhausted—and the

---

[31] *Cf.* Peter's sermon, Acts 3:19.
[32] *E.g.* Ps. 51:7; Is. 1:18; 44:22; Rev. 7:14.
[33] *E.g.* Rom. 8:1; Gal. 3:13. [34] *E.g.* Jn. 1:29.

Colossians are now in Christ, able to share in all the benefits of his substitutionary and atoning death.

Whether or not Paul had the Roman *titulus* in mind, the force of his statement cannot be evaded. The sinner is in deep trouble on account of his sins: he cannot be delivered from the rightful demands of the law. But though his own conscience might still condemn him, in Christ and for his sake, these demands have been absolutely and irrevocably set aside. Nailed with Christ to his cross they went with him to his tomb, to be buried there for ever, while Christ rose, having fully met the divine demands upon his people.

In verse 14 we seem to hear, at the cross, the authoritative word of God, as the record of man's guilt is brought before him. Our human commands, 'Wipe it off!', 'Take it away!', can give only a tiny echo of the divine decree, given before the foundation of the world, spoken finally at the death of Christ, and echoing in the hearts of all who hear and respond to the good news of God's grace.

c. *The powers were disarmed (verse 15)*

We shall be unwise to attempt to 'demythologize' this teaching of Paul's. It is not the superior enlightenment of the modern world that leads to a bland dismissal of the very idea of evil spirits. It is rather a lack of a genuine knowledge and experience of God revealed in Christ. The Spirit who baptizes us into Christ also leads us into an awareness of the spiritual warfare.[35] To know God is to be aware of the real powers of the evil one.[36] The modern ignorance of our adversary, even within the churches, is a sign of our distance from apostolic Christianity. But on the other side there is no call for the believing Christian to make too much of the 'strong man' and his armoury, since 'one stronger than he' has already appeared to overcome him and take away the weapons in which he trusts.[37] This is Paul's grand theme here. He takes us back again to the cross where the spiritual foes of mankind were 'disarmed' as Jesus had foretold.[38]

The first part of verse 15 has been understood in at least two different ways. The RSV, though criticized by some commentators, is vigorous as a picture of these evil spirit powers, these terrorists

[35] *Cf.* Mt. 3:13-4:1.   [36] 1 Jn. 5:19.   [37] Lk. 11:21-22.
[38] Jn. 12:31.

from hell, being stripped of their weapons. If God is still the subject of the sentence (as I incline to think) this version is to be preferred. If, however, the one who acts in verse 15 is Christ, then we are bound to take the meaning, more literally, to be 'He stripped himself of ...', as a person might strip his clothes from himself (the picture so often used in Paul's writings, as in 3:9). Thus the NEB translates Paul as follows: 'He discarded ... like a garment.' 'So with the powers of hell closing in on him Jesus tore them from himself.'[39]

Concerning the chief picture of verse 15 there can be no argument. The Roman triumphal procession was the best way to bring home to people that their returning generals had been winning genuine victories. No-one in town that day could possibly be ignorant of what had happened as hundreds of weary prisoners of war were paraded, straggling behind the conquering army. Shamed, and exposed to public gaze, everyone can see that there is nothing to fear from these once proud soldiers.

This splendid illustration is exactly suited to Paul's purpose. He is intent on showing that true spiritual freedom was won for all God's people through the cross of Christ. Furthermore, this is no secret to be understood and claimed by a favoured few. It is impossible for anyone to know this King and not to know his glorious victory. Freedom from demonic forces is no second or subsequent work of grace to be sought at the hands of God. It is, simply, the gospel privilege for all. For of every true believer it is written that they have already come to fullness of life in Christ, the one who is the head of all rule and authority (verse 10).

[39] Leon Morris, *The Cross in the New Testament* (Eerdmans, 1965: Paternoster, 1965), p. 229, note 52 (a quotation of G. H. C. MacGregor).

Colossians 2:16-17
Shadows and substance

THEREFORE let no one pass judgment on you in questions of food and drink or with regard to a festival or a new moon or a sabbath. 17These are only a shadow of what is to come; but the substance belongs to Christ.

Now we turn to the apostle's second warning to the Colossians: 'Don't let anyone condemn you!' It is short, but full of interest, and suggestive perhaps of the attitude of some of the visitors. It seems that there was someone among them, perhaps the leader of a team, who was openly contemptuous of the Colossian Christians. This man gave as his considered opinion (or judgment) that the church at Colossae lacked solid reality in its spiritual life, and that substantial elements, to be expected in real church life, were missing. The result of all this, needless to say, was that the visitors were confirmed in their sense of confident superiority, while the little Colossian church blushed for shame at its supposed inferiority, and felt condemned by the supercilious criticisms.

Verse 16 tells us what were the particular matters of contention between them. Verse 17 goes deeper and shows, most revealingly, the real issues at stake.

1. Particular matters of concern (verse 16)

The actual matters of concern had to do with food and drink on the one hand, and sacred times and seasons on the other. Since the language used seems to imply categories rather than particular items, we are justified in classifying the two areas of debate in more general terms. First, there are those things which

111

(according to the visitors) an authentic spirituality could not allow, and therefore must *forbid*. It simply could not do with them. Secondly, there are those things which an authentic spirituality cannot do without (so it was claimed) and therefore must *demand*. These were matters of religious obligation.

a. Things forbidden

Here, it was a matter of certain unlawful foods and drinks. As drink is mentioned, these prohibitions go beyond Old Testament regulations. So it appears that the principles of the new teachers were based on an enthusiasm for a measure of asceticism, as well as on loyalty to old patterns of spirituality.

Every Bible reader knows that Paul was no enemy of self-discipline in the life of the Christian, but rather the reverse. It is axiomatic in his portrait of the effective servant of God that appetites will need disciplining, and self-control will need to be exercised, if time is to be found for prayer, if the body is to know its master, and if the ultimate prize is to be won.[1] We also know that Paul respected the scruples of other believers in matters of abstaining from certain food and drink even when he did not share those convictions.[2] Now since Paul clearly does not approve the prohibitions of the visitors, we must assume that their teaching in this regard was not personal and voluntary, but compulsory for all who would attain spiritual perfection.

Such prohibitions Paul always regarded as false.[3] In the apostle's teaching it is sub-Christian to deny the good gifts of a bountiful Creator in the cause of an advanced spirituality. This should not need arguing with the Colossians after his exposition in the previous chapter of Christ as the source of the created order. It would be a strange road to Christlikeness to refuse the blessings that Christ had made.

As a fascinating example of Paul's dealings with immature believers tempted to move too far in the direction of asceticism, 1 Corinthians 7 repays more careful and sympathetic study than it often receives. Coming from a background in which marriage was all but obligatory, Paul justifies the unmarried state as also a good

---

[1] 1 Cor. 7:5; 9:24-27; 2 Tim. 2:5.   [2] Rom. 14:13-18.

[3] *E.g.* 1 Tim. 4:1-5. Here, as elsewhere, the Pauline authorship of the Pastoral epistles (1 and 2 Timothy and Titus) is assumed. A defence of this assumption is in J. N. D. Kelly, *A Commentary on The Pastoral Epistles* (A. & C. Black, London, 1963), pp. 30-34.

gift of God. But his approval of the celibate life is 'very sharply qualified' to use C. K. Barrett's words.[4] And from Paul there is no support whatever for the idea that refusal of marriage is a safer and quicker route to holiness. Indeed without a gift from God (Gk. *charisma*), it may well be the opposite. Paul's commendation of the single life is based on quite other grounds.

b. Things required

This second category concerned the keeping of numerous festivals and fixed celebrations as indispensable means of grace for those aspiring to sanctity.

Festival, new moon, and *sabbath* is the terminology of the Old Testament,[5] and makes a useful summary of annual, monthly and weekly celebrations. But here again it is doubtful if the visitors were content with traditional patterns. They were more thoroughgoing than that, and they were children of their own times. The fact that these sacred seasons are calendar feasts marked as yearly, monthly and weekly, strongly suggests, as Lohse puts it, that 'the sacred days must be kept for the sake of "the elements of the universe" who direct the course of the stars and thus prescribe minutely the order of the calendar'.[6]

This may be too severe on the visitors. In as much as they were Christian in their basic allegiance, they must have known that the marking of times and seasons in the Old Testament was a recognition of the authority of the Lord over the whole circle of life. But inasmuch as they recognized the authority of other powers in the heavenlies the temptation was there to stretch traditional and scriptural terms to absorb pagan content (the essence of syncretism).

Should present-day readers doubt the power of the 'elemental spirits' of paganism to influence the calendar, let them consider the English names of our own seven days of the week. Sunday is a day sacred to the sun, Monday to the moon, Tuesday to Tiw = Mars, Wednesday to Woden = Mercury, Thursday to Thor = Jove, Friday to Frig = Venus and Saturday to Saturn. With that in mind it is not difficult to understand the dilemma of those who had lived as pagans, but had recently confessed Christ as Lord.

---

[4]C. K. Barrett, *The First Epistle to the Corinthians*[2] (*Black's New Testament Commentaries*, 1971). The whole treatment of chapter 7 is fresh and thought-provoking.

[5]*E.g.* 1 Ch. 23:31.   [6]Lohse, p. 115.

Does this mean a total rejection of all other 'authorities', hence alienating one's own people, and, apparently, showing one's new faith to be intolerant and severe? Or is it possible to make the transition easier by assimilating some of the old familiar interpretations and customs into the faith of Christ?

Unfortunately it seems that the visitors had taken this second course, and had constructed a new religious calendar of fasts and feasts, based on Old Testament models, but 'enriched' as they might claim by the best 'insights' and treasures of paganism. Then the keeping of such a calendar, with its regular rhythm of festival, prayer and praise, may well have been mandatory for all who would scale the spiritual heights.

But, as we shall now see, all this found in Paul a robust opponent.

2. The issues at stake (verse 17)

This verse is one of many unforgettable statements of the Colossian letter. It defines so well the issues at stake, and shapes so clearly this part of Paul's message to the churches. And undoubtedly through this small section of the letter, the Bible speaks powerfully to us today.

The vivid contrast in verse 17 is between a *shadow* (defined by the dictionary, precisely, as 'unsubstantial') and the *substance*, real and solid. The shadow-land of verse 17a is the realm of the Old Testament. It is not to be despised because of that, but its true value lies in the future. It is a shadow of *what is to come*.

This remarkable phrase is found also in Hebrews,[7] a book very close in sympathy with Colossians. An important aim of the writer to the Hebrews is to dissuade his readers, many of whom were converted Jews, from hankering after the old forms of their religion, and persuade them to recognize the substantial and ultimate realities they now possess in their risen and ascended Lord.

So, 'what was to come' is Christ. In Paul's fine phrase, *'the substance belongs to Christ'*. *In him* is to be found all the treasures of spiritual reality and fulfilment foreshadowed in the Old Testament. To discover all that God has for his people in these last days one must be in Christ. And that is all.

[7] *E.g.* 10:1.

114

The word for 'substance' could equally well be 'body' (Gk. *sōma*). Some commentators take this to be another reference to the church of which Christ is head (in view of 1 : 18 and 2 : 19). This seems over-subtle, and is not followed by modern translations. Neither would it be so consistent with Paul's aim here which is to locate the fullness of divine truth and life in Christ alone.

We are now in a better position to assess exactly what was happening at Colossae, and to appreciate Paul's second warning to the church there.

The essential claim of the visitors we have already considered. It was to 'fill out' the understanding and experience of the young Colossian Christians. In terms of verse 17 this means that their teaching was a practical denial of the truth that 'the substance belongs to Christ'.

A *practical* denial, notice, for we have no reason to suppose that these teachers did not speak well of Christ. How else could they have won a respectful hearing at Colossae? Nevertheless they taught that even though a man was 'in Christ', for him fullness had not necessarily come.

Paul's answer is radical and striking. What, in effect, he says to the visitors is this: 'If you are still trying to "fill out" people's spiritual experience, then you are living as though Christ has not yet come. So it is *you*, with your claims to be superior, *who are still living in the shadows.'*

'Living in the shadows'. Is it possible for Christians to do this today? If so, what can it mean in practice? To answer this, we take one illustration from the letter to the Hebrews. That letter is one long appeal to the church not to return to 'shadow-land'. And the strategy of the author is the same as Paul's to the Colossians—a comprehensive exposition of the all-sufficient greatness of Jesus Christ.

It must have been a temptation for young Jewish Christians to regret the loss of the richness of the old worship. There was no room now, in the simplicity which is in Christ, for all the elaborate arrangements and regulations of the earthly sanctuary under the first covenant. But against all demands to recover such 'worship', Hebrews insists that there is no going back.

As the supreme illustration of this, the writer takes up the matter of the priesthood, that most sacred institution of the old covenant. Now, the levitical priesthood is superseded, and in

Christ and Christ alone (echoes of Colossians!), Christians have a high priest sufficient for all their needs.[8]

This high priest, Jesus Christ, first exercised his unique ministry in history, on earth, at the cross. There he offered himself as a sufficient sacrifice for all of our sins. Now he exercises his ministry in heaven, at the throne of God. It must follow therefore that the possession by the church of an active priesthood *on earth* is no longer conceivable. Trenchantly, the author writes, 'If (Christ) were on earth, he would not be a priest at all.'[9]

These are still uncomfortable words. They rebuke traditional catholic teaching on the priesthood of the apostolic ministry, just as they rebuke more generally loose talk about the ordained ministry as priesthood.

But here, once more, the substance belongs to Christ. In his unique and eternal priesthood, the solid reality of priesthood, quite beyond the range of the Old Testament levitical priesthood, exists for ever.

The question for our own day concerns what part of his priesthood Christ now shares with his people on earth. The consistent apostolic answer is that Christ's unique priestly work is untransferable to anyone on earth, and this for two reasons. First, its earthly exercise is over, finished by the sufficient sacrifice at the cross.[10] Secondly, its heavenly exercise (*e.g.* in intercession)[11] is beyond the capacities of mortal man since it demands the possession of an endless and indestructible life.[12]

This must mean that the exercise of sacrificial priesthood on earth today, however sanctioned by traditional authority, is not 'according to Christ', and must prove to be an exercise in futility, since we can have no call or competence to undertake it. Worse than that, all the patterns of 'shadow-land' begin to reappear. The importance of earthly sanctuaries, the sacred transmissible orders of priesthood, the detailed rituals of preparation, and the continual offerings that make nothing perfect, all these 'shadows of what is to come' reappear.

What Christ does unquestionably share with his people on earth are the substantial fruits of his priestly work, fruits which never 'belong to the shadows': full assurance of faith, and a heart

---

[8] Heb. 7, especially verses 23–28.   [9] Heb. 8:4–6.
[10] Heb. 10:11–12.   [11] Heb. 7:25.   [12] Heb. 7:16.

truly clean from an evil conscience,[13] with freedom now from former ways to serve the living God.[14] Here is the fulfilment of all that the prophets had said was to come, at last, substantially and really ours, in Christ.[15]

It is just this privileged access to God through Christ—this drawing near in worship[16]—that constitutes what it means to be a Christian. It is the necessary privilege of all Christian people, which they can divest themselves of, or delegate to others, only by ceasing to be fully Christian people. For this reason the whole church (and precisely not a section of it) is constituted a royal priesthood.[17]

In addition to this there is a further 'priestly' work which belongs to the whole church, and obviously cannot be exercised properly by delegation to representatives since it includes the basic elements of Christian living. This work involves the daily offering of 'spiritual sacrifices' in a life of consecration, generous giving and good deeds, as well as lips that praise God.[18] Then there is the work of evangelism in winning all people and nations to Christ: here some Christians will have special responsibilities, as Paul did,[19] yet it is evidently the responsibility of every Christian believer to see that the good news reaches every creature. For carrying out all these privileges the whole church *is* rather than *has* a priesthood. Nor can we describe the church's ministry as a representative priesthood since no Christian has liberty to appoint a representative to carry out for him these particular responsibilities.

Paul's second warning can be summarized in this way. In Christ the fullness of God's blessing for his church has come. Recognize this, and do not let anyone, however sincere (or superior) lead you back into the shadows.

One question remains. Why has it come about so often in the church's story, that people have led their fellow Christians back to 'shadow-land' in order to try to find a spiritual reality they have missed in Christ?

(i) *Is it a desire to be superior?* Re-reading verse 16 in modern versions suggests that it might have been like this with the visitors. They 'bothered' people and 'worried' them. They boldly

---

[13] Heb. 10:22. [14] Heb. 9:14 NEB. [15] Heb. 8:8–12.
[16] Heb. 7:19, 25; 10:22; *cf.* 1 Pet. 2:4. [17] 1 Pet. 2:5.
[18] Rom. 12:1; Phil. 4:18; Heb. 13:15–16. [19] Rom. 15:15–16.

'took them to task'. They called for this observance and for that. They ordered people around, perhaps on the assumption that they were the officers while the ordinary Christian were 'other ranks'. Certainly verse 17 powerfully introduces us to an equality among believers which must be unique. For since all who possess Christ have 'the substance', no Christian can have more or less. Therefore there can be no higher breed or upper class in this community. Easy to say, yet how hard we find it to live like that! There is a wish deep down in most Christian hearts to be 'more equal than others'. We like to belong to an elite corps whose job it is to direct the army to God.

(ii) *Is it false zeal?* Again it may have been so with the visitors, and there are indications of it. Zeal is a subject about which the New Testament is curiously ambivalent. It goes without saying that zeal is essential for Christian service,[20] and that by its absence a church stands condemned.[21] Yet zeal without knowledge is frequently deplored by Paul, not surprisingly perhaps in view of his experiences.[22]

False zeal is responsible for much spiritual misery. It not only denies Christians what God has not denied them,[23] and commands of them what God has not required.[24] It also promises Christians what God has not promised them. Ignorant, for example, of the intractability of sin, and God's true remedy for this, false zeal promises a freedom from imperfection that is sheer illusion. Ignorant of the purposes of God in the sufferings of this present age, it promises for 'our lowly bodies' a freedom from weakness for which Paul taught the church to wait.[25]

Only false zeal could presume to want to make the 'substance', which is Christ, more substantial still.

(iii) *Is it dissatisfaction with scriptural patterns?* Normally the 'man of the world' is spiritually satisfied and materially dissatisfied. The power of Christ turns that particular order upside down, so that, after conversion, dissatisfaction remains as a permanent mark of the Christian (Mt. 5:6).

But there is a morbid dissatisfaction that begins to question the pattern of normal Christian living in the New Testament. Such a dissatisfaction readily listens to the voice of false zeal.

This dissatisfaction (have we not all felt it?) rebels, for

---

[20] Rom. 12:11. [21] Rev. 3:15–19. [22] Phil. 3:6; Rom. 10:2.
[23] 1 Tim. 4:1ff. [24] Mk. 7:1ff. [25] Rom. 8.

instance, against the hardness of the way. It questions the toil involved in Christian service (1:24, 29); is there no better way by which God would do his work among us? It questions the effort required for prayer (4:12); is there no new level of spirituality to relieve us from the effort prayer requires? It questions the difficulty of discovering God's guidance in a complex world (1:9, 10); is there not reason to expect some more direct indications of God's will? It questions the 'sweat' of daily work (3:23); is there no higher way to find my needs met, to live 'by faith'?

However, the pattern Paul gives to the church for all these things is one that must include something of weakness, toil, hard slog, tears and anxieties.

(iv) *Is it exaggerated spirituality?* This also is revealed in verse 16. We may recognize this danger wherever there is a marked tendency to pay too little attention to the natural order ('food and drink') and too much attention to religious exercises ('festivals', *etc.*). By this false scale, the 'religious' life is specifically that without the demands of family or daily work, fully occupied in the liturgies of praise and prayer.

But this is not Paul's scale, as chapter 3 will show, with its balanced picture of true spirituality, the normal Christian life, and the whole Christian person. There is no need to return to 'shadow-land' to find reality: for in Christ, at last and finally, the substance has come.

Colossians 2:18-19
Dealing with robbers

LET no one disqualify you, insisting on self-abasement and worship of angels, taking his stand on visions, puffed up without reason by his sensuous mind, [19]and not holding fast to the Head, from whom the whole body, nourished and knit together through its joints and ligaments, grows with a growth that is from God.

Paul's third warning—'Don't let anyone disqualify you!'—exposes rather aptly the impudence of certain elements among the new enthusiasts. Through the coming of the gospel, the church at Colossae was now able to revel in a remarkable authorization, or qualification, to share the final inheritance of the saints.

Paul had gone out of his way to emphasize this at the start of the letter (1:12), no doubt to prepare the way for this note of warning. For he saw in an acceptance of the new ideas the possibility of a great evil. He recognized in the new teachers an apparent desire to 'disqualify' all other Christians who did not share their viewpoint.

This is the language of the umpire's decision. The Colossians, unlike the Galatians, were 'running well'. But suddenly authoritative voices appear on the scene declaring that, for certain reasons, their style of running is unlawful, and that the prize they were expecting will not after all be theirs. Not surprisingly the Colossians are disconcerted, begin to falter, and ask where they have misunderstood the conditions of success.

As E. F. Scott says, 'One thinks of many narrow sects since which have "disqualified" the great body of their Christian brethren because of a difference on some recondite point of custom or doctrine.'[1]

Needless to say, Paul has no intention of allowing the decision of these new self-appointed umpires to be final. The apostle will never allow that any who are 'in Christ' shall be robbed of their prize. In verse 18 he characterizes some (it could well be one) of their leaders for the spiritual scallywags they were: and in verse 19 he shows just what the result of listening to such men must be, a losing of that close relationship with Christ on which all true growth to full maturity depends.

1. Portrait of a troublemaker (verse 18)

The unusual combination of vividness and obscurity in this verse is almost certainly due to Paul's taking up the jargon of the visitors, so that he can paint them in their own colours. The commentator may hope to discern certain recognizable land-marks, but cannot possibly claim accurate identification over every detail of verse 18. To help build up what today's police call an 'identikit' portrait, we notice three main features of the kind of person Paul is describing. For the sake of simplicity we will assume that Paul has one particular person, a leading figure, in mind.

a. The specialities of his enthusiasm
b. The ground of his authority
c. The root of his trouble

a. The specialities of his enthusiasm

This man *insists on self-abasement and worship of angels.* His influence is a little more contagious than this if we understand 'insists' as 'takes delight in'.[2] 'Self-abasement' can be no ordinary kind of humility, in view of this man's evident conceit; and since the word has a nuance of mortification and self-denial, it is conceivable that we should understand it to mean 'fasting' (Gk. *tapeinophrosunē*).[3] It may be that such exercises as fasting prepared this man best for the unusual experience of worship that he treasured.

Paul nowhere forbids the early congregations to fast. At the

[1]Scott, p. 53. [2]Neil, p. 47. [3]*Cf.* Moule, p. 104.

121

same time it is of interest that we can find little in his writings that would suggest an *enthusiasm* for the practice. It is certainly permitted to Christian people.[4] But, as far as the apostle is concerned, his fasting is unavoidable,[5] and indeed one of the marks of 'weakness' by which he commends his ministry.[6] It is not possible, from New Testament evidence, to cast the apostle in the role of a keen advocate of self-imposed fasting.

Two interpretations of the strange 'worship of angels' are possible. That generally held understands from this phrase that a cult of the veneration of angels was already making its appeal to Christians, and that the visitors were enthusiastic canvassers for it. Certainly their tendency to tolerate the surrounding influences of paganism, and to look for additional spiritual mediators, gives credibility to this view. It would also link well with the 'false humility' that never can see its way boldly to approach God's throne through Christ alone (Heb. 4:11–13). This remains the more probable interpretation although there is no certain evidence of anything of the kind at this time, and it is necessary to imagine a local tendency, otherwise unrecorded.

Hesitancy to accept this interpretation will depend partly on our judgment as to how orthodox the new teachers were. That they were, unwittingly, influenced by the 'elemental spirits' we know. But this is rather different from saying that they were already praying to angels. For example, such worship of angels would have been anathema to Judaism, and we know of the strong influence of Judaism on the visitors (verse 16).

It also seems very early indeed for such heretical practices to have great appeal for the young churches. It is not until the fourth century that the Council of Laodicea forbade such prayer. Earlier, at the end of the second century, Ireneaus in *Against Heresies* gives as his testimony that the church performed nothing 'by means of angelic invocations, or by incantations, or by any other wicked curious art'. We have to ask ourselves, therefore, how likely it would be that the visitors could make much headway with this sort of thing, assuming that they believed it, as early as the third quarter of the first century.

A number of writers[7] have expressed doubts about the

---

[4] 1 Cor. 7:5.   [5] 2 Cor. 11:27.   [6] 2 Cor. 6:5.
[7] *E.g.* Zahn and P. Ewald. *Cf.* also F. O. Francis, 'Humility and Angelic Worship in Col. 2:18', *Studia Theologica*, XVI (1961), pp. 109ff.

customary interpretation and asked whether the phrase should not therefore be understood in the sense of 'worship offered by angels', so that the insistence would have been on 'angel-like' worship. It seems right to investigate this possibility in view of the lack of any solid evidence of angel worship at Colossae.

On this interpretation, the enthusiasm of the visitors and their leader would be for the way in which angels conduct their heavenly worship, and the claim might be that it was wonderfully possible to be caught up in these glorious songs through sharing the language of the angels.[8] That Paul may possibly be referring to some kind of 'angelic worship' could find some support from 3 : 16 where he gives his own positive viewpoint and instructions on spiritual worship.[9]

Whether the Colossians were being urged to venerate angels or to follow their example in the language or conduct of worship, it is significant that the enthusiasms of our man in verse 18 are hardly the enthusiasms of Paul.

b. The ground of his authority

It is recorded that the leader *took his stand on visions*. This much discussed phrase, though perplexing in detail,[10] is clear in its general meaning. This man claimed the right to be heard because of his visionary experiences. There were unhappy precedents for this in Jeremiah's time when the prophet's word was neglected in preference for the more palatable discourses of the false prophets. '"Listen to the dream I had from God last night," they say. And then they proceed to lie in my name.'[11]

What Paul himself saw, when caught up to the third heaven, he would not utter.[12] The only one to whose witness of the heavenly world Christians should listen is our Lord Jesus Christ, for he has *seen* these things. It is part of the tragic note that runs through the Fourth Gospel, and part of the tragedy of our fallen human condition, that it does not happen that way. 'Truly, truly, I say to you, we speak of what we know, and *bear witness to what we have*

---

[8] *Cf.* 1 Cor. 13 : 1. It is claimed by Lohse and other writers that a fatal objection to this interpretation is in later verses (*e.g.* 22 and 23) where the worship in question is a cult performed by men. But this overlooks the possibility that the visitors spoke of a new capacity given by the Spirit for such worship perhaps through inspired speech or song.

[9] *Cf.* below, pp. 154f.   [10] Lohse, *op. cit.* pp. 119–121 for a full discussion.

[11] Je. 23 : 25, LB.   [12] 2 Cor. 12 : 1–14.

seen; but you do not receive our testimony.[13] Worse, Christ can say to some of the spiritual leaders of his day, 'I speak of *what I have seen* with my Father, and you do what you have heard from your father.'[14] Yet, in our stupidity, we Christians have too often given credence to the words of those who claim to have had unusual visions of heavenly reality in preference to the testimony of Christ.

c. The root of his trouble
Finally Paul goes to what is the root of the trouble with this man. It is, simply, pride. 'Puffed up' is one of the old AV translations that cannot be improved upon. It exactly describes the self-important person who claims to be full of inside knowledge on spiritual matters but who is, in fact, full of wind, or as we say colloquially, hot air. Paul knew the type, and rather too many of them, through his dealings with the church at Corinth.[15]

Further, the solemn claims to special illumination are quite unfounded, quite *without reason*. The truth is that this man's convictions are not those of a spiritual mind at all, but of the mind of 'the flesh'. This is not the renewed mind so dear to Paul.[16] For is not true spiritual wisdom known by very distinctive marks that include humility and lack of boastfulness, as well as openness to reason?[17]

We now have a fairly clear picture of this disturbing character at Colossae. But one phrase is now added, and it is important. *He did not 'hold fast' to Christ the head of the church* (verse 19).

This is one of the little indications leading one to think that the new teachers were those whose original allegiance, at least, was certainly Christian. But they had not *held fast*. A rather similar situation is reported from Pergamum, according to Revelation 2:12–17. There, in most difficult days for the Christians, the majority 'held fast' to Christ's name and faith. But there were some in the church who had come instead to 'hold fast' to the teachings of Balaam and the Nicolaitans, and yet apparently remained as members of the congregation. The heavenly call to repentance shows that the Lord of the church did not think it possible for them at one and the same time to 'hold fast' to himself, and to this additional teaching.

[13] Jn. 3:11.   [14] Jn. 8; 38.
[15] 1 Cor. 8:1; *cf.* 4:18; 5:2; 2 Cor. 12:20.
[16] 3:10; *cf.* Eph. 4:23; Rom. 12:2.   [17] Jas. 3:13–18.

To listen to the visitors, then, was to risk cutting oneself off from Christ, just as this leading teacher, having found his authority (it seems) in ecstatic visions and inner mystical experiences of God, had cut himself off from Christ.

What is so significant in verse 19 is that when some of the Christians in a church lose their hold on Christ, that church loses its unity, just as at Pergamum. The 'whole body' is no longer 'knit together' as it should be. This in turn leads to a general impoverishment of church life, since the whole body should be supported and nourished with spiritual supplies from each joint and ligament.

The result of accepting the teaching of the visitors, therefore, will not be enrichment and renewal, but spiritual impoverishment and the slow drying up of true God-given resources. Did the visitors claim to have a formula for church growth? We do not know, but Paul's emphatic language here undoubtedly emphasizes *the growth that comes from God,* rather than from man.

The law of 'God's growth' for the congregation at Colossae may be expressed in simplest terms like this. *All* nourishment comes from Christ the head, and is dispensed to, and available for, every sinew and every ligament. The local church can grow only as each member or part holds fast to the head. Thus every part receives from Christ *the strength and life it supplies to the whole.*

From this, two most necessary truths may be discovered. First, each Christian has the responsibility to hold fast to Christ. This direct link between the individual believer and the heavenly Lord is one of the special glories of New Testament church life. It is a happy thing for any congregation when its members have such a relationship with Christ that they can say, 'I held him, and would not let him go.'[18] Secondly, each Christian, linked to Christ in this vital way, has some essential nourishment to give the whole body. What the Christians at Colossae needed for growth and fullness, was not the visitors and their divisive nostrums, but each other!

[18] Song 3:4.

Colossians 2:20-23
Why submit?

IF with Christ you died to the elemental spirits of the universe, why do you live as if you still belonged to the world? Why do you submit to regulations, 21'Do not handle, Do not taste, Do not touch' 22(referring to things which all perish as they are used), according to human precepts and doctrines? 23These have indeed an appearance of wisdom in promoting rigour of devotion and self-abasement and severity to the body, but they are of no value in checking the indulgence of the flesh.

This short but powerful paragraph ends the 'warning' section that began at 2:8. It forms the climax of Paul's appeal to his friends at Colossae to have nothing to do with the ideas and teaching of the newcomers. It is Paul at his most terse and trenchant.

It may be necessary for us today to take fresh note of Paul's great concern for the purity and health of the church's life. He was not frightened to speak very plainly when he saw it to be called for. Controversial issues were, in fact, the chief reason why most of his famous letters were ever written. There was none of that timidity, and false tolerance of evil, in this great defender of the gospel, that can hide under the claims of diplomacy.

So, having warned the Colossians, in three different ways, about the real character of this new teaching and its leading exponents, it is time for Paul to ask the direct and pointed questions that leap from the page on a first reading of these verses. *Why do you live as if you still belonged to this world? Why do you submit to regulations?*

The implication is that if this is the best that the new doctrine can bring, it is a poor way of life for those who have Christ.

Does this imply that some at least of the Colossians had already put themselves in the hands of the visitors and accepted their teaching? Paul's language suggests that it was so, and that a group at least had been unfaithful to their Christian beginnings. But if so, the apostle has every hope of reasoning with them and bringing them back to their senses, and to their first loyalty.

As readers of commentaries on this section of Colossians will know, it is easy to get lost in the complexity of certain textual details, especially in verse 23 where final solutions may never be possible. But the clues already given in verse 18 do help us here, and just as in that verse the general meaning was clear, even if differences over detail remain, so it is possible to discern here a consistent theme that binds the parts of this final appeal together, and makes it a fitting, and forceful, conclusion to Paul's argument.

The theme concerns slavery and freedom. Paul always saw the gospel as bringing people from slavery to freedom: and with steady eye he always saw the visitors' influence (despite their promise of 'liberation') as putting Christian people back on the road from freedom to slavery. It is this theme that illuminates this paragraph. We may set out its argument as follows.

1. The visitors cannot give freedom from the world, for they are enslaved to it.

2. The visitors cannot give freedom from the law, for they are enslaved to it.

3. The visitors cannot give freedom from the flesh, for they are enslaved to it.

1. Freedom from the world?

The religion of the visitors is essentially the religion of *the world* (verse 20). This assertion is of first importance if we are to understand the issues at stake.

Of course the world cannot do without religion. But since it rejects the truth of Christ it must find its religion elsewhere. The *elemental spirits of the universe* are glad to oblige: their leader considers himself the prince of this world,[1] and therefore is happy to provide a religion that can seem to satisfy people while keeping them from God.[2] The closer in language his religion can be to the truth, *while yet being quite different*, the better this wily prince is

[1] Jn. 12:31.   [2] 2 Cor. 11:12-15.

pleased.[3] He has his emissaries as closely involved with established religious institutions as possible.[4] His whole aim is to see that everything in his religion belongs to this world (verse 20). He discourages all eternal and imperishable concerns (verse 22). His is a religion not of faith but of sight. His ministers refuse all otherworldly teaching, and insist that people look neither up to the throne of heaven, nor beyond the practical concerns of the present day.

Since the distinctive mark of the truth of his hated enemy Christ is *grace* (1:6)—which, fortunately for him, we human beings find very humbling—so his religion is one of law, regulations, and works (verse 21), for this, he finds, is easily accepted and approved by the world.

But, says Paul, *with Christ you died to the elemental spirits of the universe*. How then can you return to live as though you belonged to this world? You have a heavenly Lord (3:1) and a heavenly hope (1:5, 27). Be glad that, *with Christ*, you have for ever been set free from this world's ideas of religion. Of course the world will not understand,[5] but how can we return from freedom to slavery now? This plain speaking will make any true Christian believer protest that he has no wish for a religion of this world. The only safety seems to lie in a faith which glories only in the cross of our Lord Jesus Christ. To trust only in that cross for the forgiveness of our sins, to know only Christ crucified as our message to the world, and daily to take up our cross, is to live as those who no longer belong to the world, nor expect to be honoured by the world.

2. Freedom from the law?

The religion of the visitors is a religion of numerous regulations (verses 20, 21). True, if these teachers were anything like other false 'freedom' preachers of Paul's day, it was probably their proud claim not only to set people free from law as a way of salvation (which indeed is Paul's gospel), but also from the law of God as the rule of the road showing Christians how to discover the will of God. Such indications as we can have in a short letter are suggestive of this. For instance, why otherwise does Paul have to say so emphatically that what God has once declared wrong is still

[3] 2 Cor. 11:1–5.   [4] Jn. 8:39–59.   [5] Gal. 4:29–31.

wrong (3:5, 6)? But church history shows that those who follow the way of antinomianism[6] soon arrive at a new and harsher legalism. Having rejected God's law, they find themselves burdened with human laws. This may have been the very plight of those who followed the lead of the visitors. The authority these men were quick to claim showed itself in a host of things 'not done' (verse 21), since spirituality was now defined as submission in everything to these new spiritual masters. Since they possessed the secret of the Lord, their word was necessarily 'law'. There is a reference in verse 22 to Isaiah 29:13, 'Their religion is but a precept of men, learnt by rote' (NEB). The full verse was quoted by Jesus when rebuking religious leaders for neglecting God's commands in the interest of their traditions. 'This people pays me lip-service, but their heart is far from me; their worship of me is vain, for they teach as doctrines the commandments of men.'[7] When the Colossians recognized this allusion it may have helped to make clear to them that the visitors' claim to be heart-to-heart with the Lord was not true.

How burdensome the rules and traditions of men have proved to be in the history of the church! But in Christ the Colossians have been freed from all this. How then can they return to such sore bondage? It is not for them now to call anyone master when Christ is Lord.

3. Freedom from the flesh?

Unhappily, the religion of the visitors is one of fleshly pride. Yet these are the very people whose special claim was to set the Colossians wholly free from the body of 'flesh'.

It seems impossible, but so, according to Paul, it was. For one thing they sought the appearance, or reputation (Lohse), of wisdom. Here were those who could claim to be experts in the spiritual life, and to have advanced in the knowledge of God beyond the run of ordinary people. Inevitably this brought them the respect of the world, which was what they really prized (contrast 1:10).

It must have seemed hard for the Colossians to accept Paul's diagnosis from the appearance of things. Were these people not marked by *rigour of devotion, self-abasement,* and *severity to the*

---

[6]Gk. *anti* (against), *nomos* (law).   [7]Mt. 15:7-9 NEB.

body? However these phrases are translated, it does not look as if these people were self-indulgent by any normal standard. Yet a closer look shows that the apostle's estimate is uncomfortably near the mark. The 'will worship' of the old version (AV) is indeed self-chosen worship ('self-inspired efforts at worship' is the JBP translation). And does not the JBP version of 'self-abasement' as 'their policy of self-humbling' carry just the right sense, that it was an activity carefully thought out in terms of its probable dividends? As for 'severity to the body', this kind of austere asceticism has always earned man's praise.

When we come to the final sentence, with its grammatical difficulties, we are left by the modern translations to decide, in general terms, between two interpretations, both available to the reader of the RSV. Of these two, the context appears to demand the particular thrust of the RSV margin, where the practices of the visitors are said to be of 'no value, serving only to indulge the flesh'. This is the choice, too, of JBP with the excellent rendering, 'But in actual practice they do honour, not to God, but to Man's own pride.' Lohse confirms this powerfully by noticing the reference, once again, to 'fullness'; so the ascetic practices 'only serve to *satiate* the flesh'.[8] Truly, it is an extraordinary turning of the tables when the apostle can claim that, so far from 'freeing' people from the flesh, these teachers are 'feeding' the flesh and teaching others to do the same.

No wonder Paul can ask the Colossians in effect, 'Why do you want to live like that? Why do you submit to men like this?' Let them hold fast the freedom of Christ, freely given to them; and let them throw off, before it is too late, the shackles of what will turn out to be a bitter and costly bondage.

To summarize the complex warnings of 2:8-23, we may say that Paul's concern is lest the Colossians lapse into a new man-made religiosity. In this sense, and only in this sense, is Paul an advocate of 'religionless' Christianity. In his own way James expresses the same concern.[9] 'Religion' as a term is not adequate to stand for the new revelation Christ has brought to the world, or the redemption believers enjoy in him. The religion of this world is just as surely condemned at the cross as the sin of the world.

The word 'religion' as it is used today can hardly be said to be a biblical word at all; it does not occur in the OT, and in the NT

[8]Lohse, p. 127.　　[9]Jas. 1:26-27.

130

there is no sanction for the modern usage. The faith of Christ is not presented as one of the 'religions' of the world, but as the unique and final truth with which no 'other gospel' may be compared (*cf.* Gal. 1:6f.).[10]

The Christian is set free from 'religion' as this world understands it, to have 'the new nature' whose life is described in chapter 3. To seek a more 'religious' life is not according to the spiritual wisdom of the apostle. Although we must be careful not to apply Paul's words in one direction only, it is understandable that Calvin should write thus on verse 23, considering the situation of his own day:

> It is of importance to consider here, how prone, nay, how forward the mind of man is to artificial modes of worship. For the Apostle here graphically depicts (lit. 'points here to the life') the state of the old system of monkhood, which came into use a hundred years after his death, as though he had never spoken a word. The zeal of men for superstition is surpassingly mad, which could not be restrained by so plain a declaration of God from breaking forth, as historical records testify.[11]

The late Professor O. Hallesby of Norway once wrote a book entitled *Religious or Christian?* It is a distinction that always demands to be borne in mind. The warnings of Paul are given to guide us today in the face of different temptations and other pressures. We may reasonably pray that we may not live 'as though he had never spoken a word'.

[10] 'Religion' in Alan Richardson, *A Theological Word Book of the Bible* (SCM Press, 1957).
[11] Calvin, pp. 203f.

Colossians 3:1–8
The Christian and Christ

IF then you have been raised with Christ, seek the things that are above, where Christ is, seated at the right hand of God. ²Set your minds on things that are above, not on things that are on earth. ³For you have died, and your life is hid with Christ in God. ⁴When Christ who is our life appears, then you also will appear with him in glory.

⁵Put to death therefore what is earthly in you: fornication, impurity, passion, evil desire, and covetousness, which is idolatry. ⁶On account of these the wrath of God is coming. ⁷In these you once walked, when you lived in them. ⁸But now put them all away: anger, wrath, malice, slander, and foul talk from your mouth.

From now on, until 4:6, the tone of Paul's letter is one of sustained exhortation. It is characteristic of the apostle's method of teaching to arrange his material in this way, and to follow an exposition of Christ and the gospel with an explanation of what it means to live in the world consistently with such truth.[1] He refuses to teach the doctrines of the faith without insisting that they be translated into corresponding behaviour and conduct.

Nor does the apostle call his hearers to a new way of life until they have understood what it means to be new persons in Christ. Paul is no mere moralist. For him there cannot be substantial goodness without godliness. If he is right here, it must follow that those standards of behaviour, and that quality of life, that we have been accustomed to describe as Christian, cannot in the end survive a serious erosion of Christian standards of belief.

[1] Rom. 12:1 and Eph. 4:1 introduce similar sections of practical exhortation.

What is satisfying about the second half of this Colossian letter is that so complete a picture of practical Christianity is given in so short a space. Here is a well-balanced description of the normal Christian life. In an ordered sequence Paul sets out five concentrated blocks of teaching, to demonstrate how the rule of Christ will shape our various relationships. Such sections of teaching material must from the earliest times have been in use for instructing young believers. But Paul is not simply taking prefabricated blocks and erecting them without shaping them to his purposes. There is nothing casual here. We shall quickly see how close and pointed are the connections between the first and second halves of this letter, for Paul the teacher knows well how to apply truth to life.

The Christian and Christ, 3 : 1-8
The Christian and the local church, 3 : 9-17
The Christian and his family, 3 : 18-21
The Christian and his daily work, 3 : 22 – 4 : 1
The Christian and the outsider, 4 : 2-6

In this chapter we shall take the first teaching block, dealing with the other blocks in the next four chapters.

The chief business of the Christian is to maintain his relationship with Christ. When this is unsatisfactory, the other relationships of life cannot succeed.

What such a relationship will require of the young Colossians, as of ourselves, is set out in four urgent commands, to each of which is attached a logical basis to show why it is so necessary that these things be done. These 'four imperatives of Christian spirituality' may be set out as follows.

1. *Seek* the things above.
2. *Set your mind* on things above.
3. *Put to death* what is earthly in you.
4. *Put away* the life you once lived.

1. Seek the things above (3 : 1)

The close connection between 2 : 20, beginning 'If with Christ you died', and 3 : 1, beginning 'If with Christ you were raised', has led some students of this letter to ask whether the exhortatory section

133

should not more properly begin at 2:20. This is a fair question, for 2:20-23 certainly was a word of exhortation and appeal based on an exposure of the new teaching and the spurious type of spirituality it offered. Paul has effectively shown that those precious preachers of 'liberty' neither enjoyed true spiritual freedom themselves nor could give it to others. His astonishment that the Colossians should think of submitting themselves to such bogus 'authorities' was well expressed by the anxious questions of 2:20.

We may be content, nonetheless, to leave the division as it is. The words of 2:20-23 are a fitting conclusion to the great 'warning' passage that began to emerge at the start of chapter 2, and was focused round the three specific warnings of 2:8; 2:16; and 2:18. Paul had said that his ministry was one of both *warning* and *teaching* (1:28). If it was insufficient to teach without warning, neither was it adequate to warn of error without teaching the right and true way. To this Paul turns at 3:1. It is wise, however, to recognize the extraordinarily close connection between this new section and what has gone before. The Colossians were not to lose their freedom by submitting to the new teachers. On the contrary they were to find and keep their freedom by *submission to the rule of Christ*.

The first imperative, 'to seek Christ', is grounded upon the fact that the Christians have been 'raised with Christ'. This vividly describes what it means to be a true believer, 'alive from the dead'. The miracle of conversion has freed the Colossians from the religious systems of their world (2:20). The distinctive mark of the new faith is that, in the old accustomed sense of the word, it is not a religion at all. It is not a human system linked to earthly sanctuaries, regulations and rites. It has no essential centre of authority in this world, for its centre is the heavenly Christ. Neither is it an exercise in interior spirituality, mysticism, or visionary enthusiasm. Set free from such subjectivism, the Christian is, simply, a man who has been granted a relationship with the exalted Christ at God's right hand. This relationship he is vigorously to pursue and develop by *seeking the things above*.

It has been customary to speak of the concerned unbeliever as a 'seeker'. But the normal biblical perspective is to see unbelievers, in relation to the things of God as characteristically seeking after either 'wisdom', or 'signs', as means of establishing their own righteousness before God.[2] These searches are not likely to succeed! In biblical teaching there is no human 'search for God'; the story is, from the beginning, that of a divine search for those who hide from their Maker.[3] When men and women begin their search for God and his forgiveness, it is evidence of a prior work of God. Having found that forgiveness, or been 'found' by the heavenly Father,[4] the search for reconciliation is over.

But this, significantly in view of Paul's over-all answer to the new teaching, is the beginning of a daily seeking after the things above. Thus the apostle guards his teaching against the charge of complacence. The Christian is one constantly looking upwards (spatial concepts are a *sine qua non* of apostolic Christianity) and drawing close to the throne of grace.

Underlying this description of Christ as seated at God's right hand is Psalm 110:1, the messianic prophecy most often quoted in the New Testament. Christ is now victorious over all the powers and principalities that would keep us from God. In union and fellowship with this Lord, the Christian is set free *from* the tyranny of the 'elemental spirits', and *for* the perennial enjoyment of God's presence. Now, nothing can hold him to the unsatisfying shadows of 'religion'.

It is this present access to God's presence, in and through Christ, which is the open secret at the heart of this great verse. The believer is now acceptable to God and welcome in Christ's name. Here he may take his stand,[5] and here be perfectly 'at home'. Living in Colossae, the Christian also lives in *Christ*. Both are 'home' to him. Just as, whenever business trips might take the Colossian believer away from the Lycus valley, he would always be anxious to get back to his family, so he is always eager to approach his Lord in heaven and enjoy the blessings of his presence.

To seek the things above, then, takes us to the very summit of Christian experience in this life. It is daily to hold fast to Christ as the centre and source of all our joys. It is to enter his gates with praise and come into his courts with thanksgiving. Everywhere the Psalms express the joy of this experience.

> How dear is thy dwelling-place
> thou Lord of Hosts

[2] 1 Cor. 1:22; Rom. 10:3.   [3] Gn. 3:9; Lk. 19:10.
[4] Lk. 15:24.   [5] Rom. 5:2.

135

> I pine, I faint with longing
> for the courts of the Lord's temple;
> my whole being cries out with joy
> to the living God.
> Even the sparrow finds a home,
> And the swallow has her nest,
> where she rears her brood beside thy altars,
> O Lord of Hosts, my King and my God.
> Happy are those who dwell in thy house;
> they never cease from praising thee.[6]

2. Set your minds on things above (3:2-4)

In this second great 'imperative' of true spirituality, the difference between the old version (AV) and the RSV is important. The call to the Colossians is not simply that they should 'set their affections' on the things of Christ; for that is the essence of the first 'imperative'. Here Paul tells of the need to use the renewed *mind*. He calls the Christians to come to a true understanding of the heavenly Christ, so that they may discern his will and purposes.

But we are not likely to see the full significance of this second 'imperative' until we study the logical basis for it, given in verses 3 and 4. This reasoning is introduced by the important negative of verse 2b. The Colossians are *not* to set their minds to a consideration of the things that are on earth.

Does this mean that 'things temporal' are to have none of their attention? In view of what follows this is an impossible interpretation. Taken like this, Paul would be advising them to have nothing to do with this life at all. He would be teaching that the activities of human life can never occupy the sustained and serious attention of the Christian. But is such heavenly 'absent-mindedness' really what the apostle orders? If so, it would be out of the question for a 'spiritual' person to devote himself to practical affairs. He could take no part in activities where concentration on the matter in hand is essential. A Christian could never be a mechanic, a surgeon, a businessman, or a chef; or even a good husband, wife, employer, *etc.* as Paul expounds later. As for teaching and nursing, or minding the baby, such lack of attention would get what it deserves. No, read superficially in this way, verse 2

[6] Ps. 84:1-4 NEB.

would be a recipe for pseudo-spirituality of a kind that harms the cause of Christ.

The 'things on earth' (Gk. *epi tēs gēs*) receive another mention in verse 5 as *what is earthly* (Gk. *epi tēs gēs*) *in you*. Therefore these earthly things must certainly include the sins that are to be mortified. And the first step in such mortification, as every Christian knows, is not to set the mind upon them.

This is perhaps sufficient explanation of these words: it is fundamental to apostolic teaching that we cannot set our minds on Christ and sin at the same time, and that to concentrate on such earthly things is seriously to enfeeble, and even threaten, our fellowship with Christ. Yet verse 2 is not to be thought of as self-explanatory. There may well be significance in the close line of reasoning that links verse 2 with the intriguing language of verses 3 and 4.

Verse 3 describes the great change that has taken place for the Colossians through their regeneration. The old life is over and the new life has begun. The source of this new life is in Christ: it is in union and fellowship with the exalted Christ that they have found the great secret of the knowledge of God.

Why is this new union with Christ said to be 'hidden'? The reason for this is that the perfect union between Christ and his people is a heavenly union, and therefore *is* hidden from man's observation. What can be seen of it on earth is the church militant, no doubt, but it is also the church frail and very human. Despite worldwide achievements in people's hearts, (1:6) the church continues to bear the marks of weakness and humiliation. It is often cold (Ephesus), slandered and imprisoned (Smyrna), in part faithless (Pergamum), tolerant of the intolerable (Thyatyra), lifeless and sleepy (Sardis) and wretchedly self-satisfied (Laodicea).[7]

There is comfort here as well as shame. For if the 'body' is marked by humiliations, so in his earthly ministry was the 'head', though himself without sin. Identifying himself with sinners, he was 'made sin' for us.[8] How impossible for the man and woman of the world to see the glory of God in the man on the cross!

This is exactly where verse 4 completes the story. A day is coming when the Christ of faith whom we now worship will be the Christ revealed for what he is to the astonished gaze of all mankind. Then the church universal will be revealed for what it is,

---

[7] Rev. 2 and 3: the seven churches of Asia.   [8] 2 Cor. 5 :21.

also to the astonishment of the world. Christ will then be so united with his people that the glory manifested by him will be manifested by them also.

But all this lies in the future, and in marking this fact Paul gives an intentional caution. Though it is wonderfully true now that 'Christ is our life', the visible manifestation of this (in a reality that is undeniable) lies outside present possibilities. The steady transformation described in 2 Cor. 3:18 therefore has real limitations. Divine glory is not now to be seen unmistakably on earth, either in the life of the church corporately, or in the experience of Christians individually. This means that while it is scriptural to speak of ourselves being united with Christ in heaven, it is unsafe to speak of the exalted Christ being so joined to us on earth that his will becomes ours, his actions our actions, and even his words our words. The Spirit takes of the things of Christ and declares them to us; he ministers to us of the grace and gifts of Christ. But he does not bring Christ down from heaven.

Yet it is this egregious error that has caused misunderstanding and grief again and again in church history. It is heard, for example, when the church is regarded, in too literalistic terms, as an 'extension of the incarnation', and the claim made that Christ is so joined to his church on earth that its teaching becomes his teaching, and its traditions an expression of his mind. Individually it is heard in the claims of fanaticism. When the phrase 'Christ is our life' is interpreted to mean that in the person fully possessed by the Spirit, the very life of Christ is lived out through him, so that he may have the power and wisdom to do on earth all that Christ did, then we hear the very claims that it is Paul's purpose here to rebut.

The apostle's teaching is that this new life of theirs, this spiritual reality which is now the possession of the Colossians by the creative power of God, is *hid with Christ in God*. This remarkable phrase means that the gift of salvation, like all other spiritual treasure, is located now in Christ (2:3) and is ours only *by faith*. This life 'is and remains totally bound to Christ and is not at man's disposal ... (it) is hidden with Christ in God, removed from the view of man, and it cannot be tangibly exhibited'.[9] Christians daily enjoy and experience this life in Christ, and its power is seen just in so far as they live under the rule of grace. Its

[9] Lohse, pp. 133–135: the whole discussion is illuminating.

proper manifestation on earth is a life rightly lived in the fivefold relationships described in this entire section. Its power is seen in a holy life, a united congregation, a happy Christian home, a situation at work that reveals something of the Spirit of Christ, and in effective witness to the outsider. It is in this, and only in this way, that we can reflect Christ's glory on earth today.

This may give us still more insight into the instructions of verse 2. First, the negative: we are *not* to set our minds on earthly things. Several commentators[10] have drawn attention to the only other use of this phrase in Philippians 3 : 19, where Paul describes certain sensualists and gourmets known to him (presumably professing Christians), who with their minds thus 'set on earthly things' revealed themselves to be enemies of Christ's cross.

No-one has suggested that the visitors to Colossae made a god of the delights of the table. But it may well have been that they laid great emphasis on 'spiritual' feasting. Did they complain about the plain fare, the ordinary bread of life, as dry and unexciting, and declare that it was possible to enjoy more intoxicating provision at God's table?

This is not to say that Paul had no rich spiritual fare to offer, or that he denied the spiritual joys of an overflowing heart (3 : 16). What he seems concerned to say is that these will not be found without setting the mind on *heavenly* things. To seek for Christ in his church on earth, or in the human heart, is to be looking in the wrong place. This is not to forget the indwelling of the Holy Spirit when, by faith, we may know Christ dwelling with us. But it is to deny that the Holy Spirit makes the church or the Christian so fully the place where Christ is to be found that we may seek from church or Christians on earth the sure and certain manifestation of Christ. No! To look within must in the end mean a fresh discovery of sin, not the Saviour. Only on the last day when Christ returns will his church be so perfectly and purely united with him that it will appear actually to be what it already is in the divine purpose.

So, finally, we come to the positive instruction, the second all-important 'imperative' of the spiritual life. Christians are to set their minds on the things above. This is the call for the use of the Christian's renewed mind in the continued contemplation of the ascended Christ. Christ is the one whom we love to seek for

[10] *E.g.* Abbott, p. 228.

himself, to praise with overflowing heart, the one we are content simply to be with. He is also one whom now we must get to know. What are his likes and dislikes? What pleases him (1:10)? Who is he and what does this mean for the world, and for us (1:15-22)? What is there about him that we need to know if we are to grow to maturity (1:28)?

Paul very often urges the young Christian to think in this way. It is a mark of spiritual consecration to do so, and it is the normal way in which to discover the will of God for our lives.[11] For the apostle, the ways of paganism are explicable only because of ignorance.[12] And the new way of life, pleasing to God, can be discovered only by true knowledge.[13]

The direction of our constant meditation is not inwards, as we have seen, but upwards. Only in this way are we saved from the deceitful perils of subjectivism. By setting our minds on the things above, we begin to know our Lord so well that it becomes increasingly clear how to live worthily for him in the world of affairs. Mind and conscience are so informed that we recognize the way in which to walk, to right or to left, and we are able to teach one another with ever-increasing certainty. The more we set our minds to consider the things above, the firmer the ground beneath our feet. 'Because "to consider" demands sobriety, every kind of reckless enthusiasm is rejected.'[14]

In the New Testament, a sober mind is an essential concomitant to a fervent spirit.[15] Without it we can find ourselves at the mercy of what are normally unreliable signposts, such as a sense of peace, a spiritual compulsion or inward leading, or some visionary experience. Without it our frail ship may easily be blown off course by every new wind of doctrine.[16] Without it we still think like a child in spiritual matters,[17] being yet unskilled in the word of righteousness.[18] We can begin to walk the way of safety and true Christian spirituality only when we set our minds with diligence on the things above.

3. Put to death what is earthly in you (3:5-6)

The first imperative of Christian spirituality concerned an individual's personal devotion to Christ: the second his study and

---

[11]Rom. 12:2.   [12]Eph. 4:17-19.   [13]Eph. 4:20-25 *et seq.*
[14]Lohse, p. 133.   [15]*E.g.* 1 Pet. 1:13.   [16]Eph. 4:14.
[17]1 Cor. 13:11.   [18]Heb. 5:13.

growing understanding of the will and purposes of Christ.

For his next imperative Paul concentrates on these earthly things already introduced. Having resisted a pious subjectivism, Paul now asks the Christians what it is they discover when they search their hearts. The result of this self-examination is disconcerting, as verse 5 shows, and necessarily leads immediately to a third imperative.

It is impossible to admire too much the sanity of this apostolic teaching. Since the very straightforwardness of the language may lead us to neglect the deeper implications of what Paul says, a number of observations may help to show the permanent value for the church of the third imperative.

(i) *Outside Christianity, the essential link between religion and righteousness is never finally and securely forged.* In the apostles' teaching, those called to a knowledge of God are, by that very fact, called to holiness. The foundations for this teaching lie deep in the Old Testament revelation, being one of its chief glories. In short, they who love the Lord, hate evil.[19] What better illustration of this principle could we have than 3 : 1–8? Seeking the Lord, and mortifying what is earthly in us, go together.

(ii) *Apostolic teaching is always explicit and unambiguous about the extent of evil in the human heart.* This fits in with the teaching of Christ,[20] which is the same thing as saying that it fits the facts. The gross sins of verse 5 are precisely those sins of paganism which Judaism always held in horror. Yet Paul says that the roots of these sins lie so deep in all of us that they cannot wholly be eradicated, even from the hearts of the redeemed. Paul tells the Christian, rejoicing in a new relationship to Christ (1 : 12–14), that if he looks within, he will discover just what is earthly in him, that is, the seeds of evil, vile things. Yes, even in the heart of the established Christian are the makings of an idolater. Was Paul not right?

(iii) *Apostolic teaching on mortification is severely practical.* Of course it has little to do with severity to the body (2 : 23); mortification of the flesh in that sense easily leads to an un-Christian denial of human sexuality and all natural appetites. Nor is the flesh made inactive or powerless to trouble us by passive or interior acts of faith. We can reckon these vigorous roots to be dead only at the risk of self-deception. Not until death shall we be

[19] Ps. 97 : 10 margin. [20] Mk. 7 : 14–23.

free from 'evil desires'. What Paul demands is that the Christian deals so ruthlessly with these things, in thought and deed, that no unworthy actions mar his testimony.

> We are frequently told that what matters is not what we say, or what we do; it is what we are. If that means that motive and intention are all-important, it is, of course, entirely true. But if it means that we are to judge ourselves, or that God judges us, by our present dispositions, and not by our actual output in word and deed, I must deny it altogether ... If our Lord does not teach that we shall be judged by our works, it is indeed hard to say what he does teach. The fact is that the characters with which we begin are very largely inherited ... We must treat them, like the outward circumstances of our lives, as difficult material with which in union with God we are called faithfully to deal. God judges us, and we must judge ourselves, by the way in which we do actually deal with them ... Let us take care of our conduct, and our characters will in the long run take care of themselves.[21]

(iv) *The imperatives of the New Testament are always well supported with incentives.* Christians often know what is required of them, but lack the desire to do it. Attempts to stir them emotionally have no lasting effects. Paul never 'shouts louder' so that we may obey him. He well knows that his third imperative makes great demands. Pressures from within and without threaten a steady obedience. Incentives are desperately needed, and so we are given them. The 'therefore' of verse 5 points back to verses 1–4. Devotion to Christ will be badly spoiled by the practices of verse 5. And does not a growing knowledge of Christ, and his will, show just how displeasing to him, and unworthy of him, such things are? And have we not the great incentive of his 'appearing'?[22] If that is not enough, Paul surrounds the imperative with one more inducement to pure and holy living. Looking into the future we see that something else is coming, the judgment of God, which will be visited on just such things. As well as the promise of verse 4, we need, as the Colossians needed, the warning of verse 6.

[21] H. L. Goudge, *The Pastoral Teaching of St Paul* (Edward Arnold, 1913), pp. 40–42.
[22] 1 Jn. 3:2–3.

(v) *The ethical teaching of the apostles is never out of date.* Today the call is often heard for an updating of apostolic teaching to meet the needs of the modern world. How often we speak of the speed at which our world changes! The older pastor wonders if he can speak to the situation of young people today, so different in countless ways from that when he was their age. How much less can Paul speak, over a gap of nineteen centuries, to modern youth! Yet the teaching of this third imperative shows certain ways in which human nature and human society have hardly changed in all that time.

Licentiousness and avarice were the marks of human society in Paul's day. And, as the power of Christian truth declines, so they resume their ancient sway in our own society. These are still the forces by which people rule their lives. What reason, then, have we to cease to listen to the apostle's teaching? Does not Paul still speak exactly to our need?

4. Put away the life you once lived

The third imperative had to do with 'evil within', the plague of the human heart. The fourth imperative has to do with evil ways inherited from the past, the pagan lifestyle from which the Colossians had been redeemed. With regard to such things the Christians are told to *put them all away.*

The force of this final imperative of Christian spirituality may be better appreciated if set out in two propositions.

(i) The old way of life is to be decisively *challenged.*
(ii) The old way of life is to be decisively *changed.*

(i) The ways in which communities have lived together in days past are traditional, and treasured because of it. The old tribal or social customs, the 'ways inherited from your fathers',[23] are, to a greater or lesser extent, binding on succeeding generations. Inasmuch as these are not lived under the rule of Christ, Paul sees them as necessarily under the judgment of God. When people are turned to Christ, it is inevitable that they should bring all their past to him for acceptance or rejection. The validity of old habits, conventions and manners is challenged. However time-honoured

[23] 1 Pet. 1:18.

they may be, with the coming of Christ, and the start of discipleship, this is inescapable.

But it is also unpopular! For instance, it is all but taken for granted by the popular mind of our day that Christian missionaries should be criticized for having upset the social structures and religious customs of primitive peoples. It is asked by what authority they have challenged these ancient ways of life. The answer to this must be, by the authority of Christ! That is not to assume that the work of Christian missions has been without fault: but it is to say that the rule of Christ is an essential part of the gospel which God has commanded to be carried to every nation under heaven.

The Colossians, then, must challenge their past in the name of Christ. That is what baptism means. The serious consequences of not doing this will be the almost unconscious assimilation into the life of the church of parts of their pagan inheritance. This kind of adulteration of gospel truth is what Paul had recognized in the newcomers. That is why he is so insistent that the Colossians should make a clean break with their past.

(ii) Verse 8 is characteristic of apostolic Christianity.[24] Paul, in particular, is constantly impressing on the young churches the need to have done with the old non-Christian ways of life.[25] *Once*, such things were understandable: *but now* they are out of the question for those who know Christ.

The enormous moral change brought about at the beginning by the preaching of the gospel can be glimpsed in such a passage as Ephesians 4:17 – 5:14. The new Christians followed a completely different way of life from that of their pagan neighbours. The difference that conversion makes will not, of course, be so marked in a culture which has been impregnated with Christian truth and standards over many generations.

Even so, people never face a bigger moral revolution than when first they acknowledge Christ. We may recognize here another of Paul's implied criticisms of the teaching of the newcomers with their grandiose descriptions of the change the blessing of sanctity would bring (*cf*. 2:11). Can anything be comparable, in moral terms, to the great change described as leaving the powers of darkness and living in the realm of light?

What then are the young Christians to 'put away' so decisively?

[24] *Cf*. 1 Pet. 2:1.   [25] *E.g*. Rom. 13:12.

Five sins are catalogued in verse 8 (as in verse 5). It goes without saying that they are chosen with great care. They are precisely the sins of speech that make harmonious human relationships impossible. Such evils were at the heart of pagan society,[26] as it is these very things which destroy every dream of human brotherhood today. And the Colossians would have to acknowledge that anger, rage, malice, slander and abusive talk (not 'filthy talk' which breaks the sequence of speech that is *divisive*) had characterized life as they had known it.

This theme is beautifully chosen to conclude the first section (verses 1–8), and introduce the second (verses 9–17). The four imperatives of Christian spirituality focus around the Christian's relationship to Christ himself. But such a relationship never stands alone. By being drawn close to Christ, the Christian is drawn close to all others who love and seek the same Lord. Union with Christ must lead to unity in the congregation: and to that great subject the apostle is now to address himself. As he knows, Christians do not always live as they ought with their fellow believers, even along the lines he has just mentioned.[27] But the chief concern in his mind is the threat to unity posed by the visitors. For the apostle, it was clear that the effect of their teaching was not only to keep believers from developing their personal relationships with Christ in a healthy way, but also to damage the prospects of unity among themselves. So to this matter of their relationships with one another he now turns.

[26] *Cf.* Rom. 1:29–30.　　[27] *E.g.* 2 Cor. 12:20.

Colossians 3:9-17
The Christian and the local church

D O not lie to one another, seeing that you have put off the old nature with its practices [10]and have put on the new nature, which is being renewed in knowledge after the image of its creator. [11]Here there cannot be Greek and Jew, circumcised and uncircumcised, barbarian, Scythian, slave, free man, but Christ is all, and in all.

[12]Put on then, as God's chosen ones, holy and beloved, compassion, kindness, lowliness, meekness, and patience, [13]forbearing one another and, if one has a complaint against another, forgiving each other; as the Lord has forgiven you, so you also must forgive. [14]And above all these put on love, which binds everything together in perfect harmony. [15]And let the peace of Christ rule in your hearts, to which indeed you were called in the one body. And be thankful. [16]Let the word of Christ dwell in you richly, teach and admonish one another in all wisdom, and sing psalms and hymns and spiritual songs with thankfulness in your hearts to God. [17]And whatever you do, in word or deed, do everything in the name of the Lord Jesus, giving thanks to God the Father through him.

In the sustained exposition of what it means to live under the rule of Christ (beginning at 3:1), the five sections are quite recognizable: the demarcation lines are also clearly marked, with one possible exception. The boundary between the first and second sections is not immediately obvious. Here, the second section on the Christian's relation to his fellow Christians is taken to begin at verse 9, a decision that must by judged later by the success or otherwise of the interpretation that follows.

All that Paul here urges upon the Colossian believers depends upon his basic assumptions concerning the nature of the church. A careful study of the language he uses will show that he sees the church as the 'new creation', a renewed society requiring a fresh way of living (9–11). Here there cannot be the same divisions the world knows since *Christ is all, and in all.* Paul also commandeers the age-old titles of Israel, *God's chosen ones, holy and beloved,* in order to complete the picture of this new society, for he sees the church as the 'new Israel' where a standard of mutual love is demanded as befits God's people on earth (12–13).

In a letter that has superlative things to say about Christ, it is no surprise to find superlative things said about his church. And that, not in some ideal form such as 'the blessed company of all faithful people', but of the actual, visible, local churches existing in Colossae or Laodicea; yes, even of the congregation meeting in the house of the good lady Nympha (4:15–16).

1. The new creation

The new creation, then, is a society where the barriers that separate us from one another in this world are abolished (verse 11). *Here there cannot be* the deep divisions, national and traditional, tribal and geographical, social and cultural, that largely distinguish us from one another. It is a marvellous dream. But, in practical terms, what a risky claim to make! Can it begin to reveal itself as reality? It is no surprise to the Christian, with his knowledge of the extent of man's ruin through the fall, to see, again and again, that liberal optimism concerning the speedy establishment of multiracial societies is not borne out by the bitter facts of experience. But have the churches always seemed to have that evident position of superiority in what is now called 'race relations' that could make their message to the world more acceptable or credible?

In this situation Paul has only one hope. It is Christ and his reconciling power (*cf.* 1:20). The dream of breaking down the walls of separation can be earthed only when, among a given community of people, *Christ is all, and in all.*

Christ is all means, simply, that Christ is all that matters. Yet there is evident reference here to the troubles at Colossae. It was not going to be sufficient to bind them together in an unbreakable unity so that Christ should be *in all* God's believing people. It was

147

also necessary that Christ should be 'all in all' to each member of the church, sufficient to supply every need for living and teaching, if true spiritual unity was to be maintained. Only if, in the vivid phrase of 1 Corinthians 15:28, Christ was 'everything to everyone' could community bonds be strong enough to hold them all within one fellowship.

There is nothing glib here. Paul well knew the almost unbridgeable gulfs that exist between human beings. How can slave and master find common ground? Or the uncouth Scythian from northern Greece relate to the sophisticated freeman of Athens? But Paul is convinced of the power of Christ, not to bring people together while remaining just what they were before, but to change them so that a genuine meeting of mind and heart is achieved. Obviously the Jew cannot remain the person he was if Christ becomes *all* to him; nor will the proud Greek debater any more mock at the finality of the resurrection.[1]

In short, this kind of Christian unity is the result of genuine spiritual revolutions in individual lives, where *the old nature* with all its prejudices and hatreds is *put off*, and *the new nature put on*. This is the language of regeneration, or as Paul describes it here and elsewhere,[2] new creation. Not that Paul teaches Christian people simply to rest in that mighty initial work of deliverance (1:13), for the God who began his work in them continues it by constant renewal[3] as they increase steadily towards mature knowledge (1:9), and so grow to be more like Christ who is the image of God (1:15), their creator.

In this local assembly of united individuals (I almost said 'nations'), the language spoken must, of course, be that of truth. These believing people now meeting and living together cannot now *lie to one another*, in view of all that God has done for them individually and corporately. Just why 'lying lips' is chosen to characterize the kind of behaviour that should now be unthinkable is probably due to the link with verse 8. Those things that the Christian must *put to death* and *put away* are precisely those sins that destroy, not only individual integrity, but the very possibility of social harmony as well (verses 5–8). Verse 8 therefore becomes a most interesting bridge between the first two sections. For it is in genuinely seeking Christ and fellowship with him (and thus avoiding all that displeases him) that we discover the possibility

---

[1] Acts 17:18, 32.   [2] 2 Cor. 5:17.   [3] *Cf.* 2 Cor. 4:16.

of real fellowship with *one another* (this tell-tale little phrase now appearing several times in this section, and nowhere else: verses 9, 13, 16).

The difficulty of establishing viable human relations without truthfulness may not be obvious to those brought up in a culture that has been deeply influenced by Christianity. In such a culture, whatever our personal habits may be, there is still all around us a general acknowledgment of the claims of truth. But to embark on, say, business dealings with those who have never known the constraining force of such general acknowledgment can be a bewildering experience. The same is true, so I am told, in the educational field when dealing with young Marxist teachers for whom the sacredness of the cause makes other truths negotiable.[4] Some reminiscences of Anders Nygren, from his experiences in the 1930s, illuminate this theme.

In this context I think particularly of my friend Birger Farell, minister of the Swedish congregation in Berlin, who made his home a refuge and meeting place for many persecuted Germans. Through him I was able to meet many of the leading opponents of Hitler and even occasionally take part in their meetings. Since the Germans had officially no freedom of speech, I felt it incumbent upon me to speak in their stead, and in this connection visited various German ministries, a remarkable experience. In the Ministry for Interior Affairs I received a concrete example of the new Nazi concept of truth, that is, 'Truth is what is to the advantage of your own people.' The official who received me outlined the new situation, but all that he said was what we ordinary mortals called untrue. When in the course of our conversation he realized that I was well acquainted with the situation, his whole approach changed. He accepted my point of view and tried as far as possible to put things in a favourable light. He seemed no whit troubled by his

[4] 'A student ... active in the Young Communist League and a member of the YCL committee, returned home after a YCL meeting. He had a feeling of disgust. At the meeting there had been lies, intrigues, and vile bureaucratic phraseology that no one believed. Suddenly he remembered seeing a little book, a gospel, that his parents had owned. By the time he finished reading it, he was already a Christian. Here he found what the Young Communist League could not give him: truth.' From an interview with Anatoli-Krasnov-Levitin conducted by Derek Sangster in *Christianity Today*, 23 June, 1978.

149

'double-think', and indeed why should he? Measured by the new concept of truth he had spoken the truth both times. If a foreigner, who apparently knows nothing, should come, it is 'to the advantage of your own people' to pull the wool over his eyes. If it appears he is well acquainted with the situation, it is 'to the advantage of your own people' to try to put things in as favourable a light as you can. From such negotiations one returned with an increased affection for our old honest concept of truth.[5]

2. The new Israel

Long ago God had chosen Israel to be 'a people for his own possession, out of all the peoples that are on the face of the earth', and 'set his love upon' them for no other reason than that 'the Lord loves you'.[6] In so singling them out, God called Israel to be 'a holy nation'.[7] Now Paul can take the characteristic titles of Israel, the 'chosen', 'holy', and 'beloved' people and boldly give them to the local community of Christians in Colossae. The fact that this transfer of Israel's titles to the church is almost a commonplace in the New Testament[8] shows the revolution in thinking that had taken place in Paul's mind. His meeting with Christ had transformed his whole understanding of God's plan for the world. What then are the qualities now to be expected of God's people? Why, the very qualities which, long ago, they had come to recognize and understand in God himself through his election of them, namely *compassion, kindness, lowliness, meekness, and patience.* 'All the five terms that describe the new man's conduct are used in other passages to designate acts of God or of Christ.'[9] The acts of God that revealed those divine qualities *par excellence* show us just what will be needed to bring the blessings of the new covenant to weak and sinful people, and to maintain their cause despite repeated offences and backsliding.

'If God so loved us, we also ought to love one another.'[10] It is this invariable New Testament demand that Paul makes here of the Colossians. They must *put on*, or clothe themselves with, the

[5] *The Philosophy and Theology of Anders Nygren* edited by Charles W. Kegley (Southern Illinois University Press, 1970), p. 21.
[6] Dt. 7:6-8.   [7] Ex. 19:5-6.
[8] *E.g.* Rom. 8:33; Phil. 3:3; 1 Pet. 2:9; Jas. 1:1; Rev. 1:6.
[9] Lohse, p. 147.   [10] 1 Jn. 4:11.

moral characteristics just mentioned, so that they can act toward others as God in Christ has acted towards them. This can only mean that they are bound to be *forbearing* to *one another*, despite many a provocation, and, *if one has a complaint against another*, then the right course is clear from the Lord's dealings with them: *as the Lord has forgiven you, so you also must forgive* (verse 13).

In describing the local church as an example of the new creation and the new Israel, Paul supplies us with two revealing and exciting clues as to what it means to be a Christian.

First, in the original creation God's supreme purpose was to make man in his own image; but through Adam's sin this human nature was marred and spoiled. In the new creation God is remaking men and women to be part of a new human society. In the local church we should be able to discern what it means to be a proper human being. Since, for Christians, Jesus alone can be the one true Man perfectly revealing the image of God, so to be recreated in Christ and renewed constantly after God's image is to rediscover the road to true human-ness.

It is important to recognize a clear implication of this: *there is nothing inhuman in the nature of genuine Christian spirituality*. If, as we suspect, the visitors were purveying a form of that super-spirituality which troubles the church in every age (*e.g.* 2:23), there is a strong corrective here in Paul's teaching. Holiness is to be recognized not by religious achievements or by a spirituality that is superior to the normal human condition, but by the development of a genuine human-ness, by a freedom that is unafraid to be, in Christ, the person God made us.

Secondly, in the making of Israel God was calling a people to himself to be specially his own, revealing by their obedience the divine character and purposes. So to be part of the new Israel is a call to the Colossians to demonstrate the family likeness by imparting to others what they had themselves received. *As the Lord has* (for example) *forgiven you, so also you must forgive* (verse 13) is one of the regulative principles of living, according to the New Testament.[11]

To summarize both the examples, it is God's purpose that in the local church should be seen a glimpse of the new man, and through this, a glimpse too of the God in whose image he was made, and by whose grace he has been redeemed.

[11] *E.g.* Lk. 6:36–38; Jn. 13:14, 34; Eph. 5:1–2.

3. Unity in the local church

We now return to the main theme of the whole section. The appeals for open truthfulness with one another, and for a spirit of forgiveness and mutual tolerance, sharply demonstrate Paul's concern for unity in the local church, a concern which governs all that he writes from verse 9 to verse 17. Miss this, and we read the paragraph in vain.

As usual it seems that the apostle has his eye on the visitors and their divisive influence. The result of their activities must inevitably lead to some kind of disunity. We have already seen the main cause of this in their demand for a second initiation to complete the work begun at conversion/baptism. Through this further crisis of faith the believer leaves the life of barrenness and wilderness experience, and enters a new land of promise, flowing with milk and honey. After such an experience, fellowship with the local church seems tame and insipid; it becomes necessary to withdraw with like-minded 'spiritual' people for a 'deeper' experience of fellowship.

Whatever form this search for 'fullness' took, there could not fail to be, within it, perhaps hardly realized or acknowledged, an implicit criticism of the credentials of the local congregation of believers. Here, surely, lies the reason why the apostle takes pains to name the local church, with all its faults, as a true representative of the new creation and the new Israel. And if Paul is right, there cannot be any more privileged group to join. To withdraw from this is not to find something richer and better, but to cut oneself off from the fellowship of God's own people.

Once again we owe to the apostle a real liberation, this time from those overstrained demands for a community that looks more like an outpost of heaven on earth as we think it ought to be; and we can at last humble ourselves to recognize that the treasure of Christ's Spirit resides in the very ordinary clay of the local congregation of his people in Colossae, as elsewhere.[12] Once again we learn from him that it is in Christ, and through him alone, that we are already qualified to share in the communion and fellowship of the saints (1:12).

The sub-section verses 9 to 13 appears to be complete in itself, with its two fine descriptions of the church as a new (we might say 'alternative') society which by its very nature demands of its

---

[12] *Cf.* 2 Cor. 4:7–12.

members that they live in unity and godly love together. That Paul does not end this section here is a sign of how much on his mind was this issue of Christian unity. Not that the churches of the Lycus valley alone were threatened with dissension; other 'prison epistles' such as Ephesians and Philippians contain sustained pleas for unity. Nevertheless the call to close ranks and stand firm together (*e.g.* 1:23) is well marked in the Colossian letter. So here Paul writes additional pleas for unity, passionately felt, but also very carefully shaped, to make maximum impact on the precise situation in Colossae following the coming of the visitors.

a. Above all ... put on love (verse 14)

This will act as a bond, a word that 'means the fastening together of separate items which are thus brought together into a unity'.[13] It is in this harmony that the Colossian believers will find 'completion' or 'perfection'. Here, surely, we pick up echoes of the new propaganda with its probable leanings to perfectionism. Was it suggested that 'perfect love' could best be found in a new fellowship of those who looked for this fuller experience? Whatever the precise nature of the visitors' appeal, Paul's answer is applicable to all such tendencies to elitism. True Christian love does not seek its own, least of all a more heavenly fellowship of the like-minded, but must give itself in humility to the very heterogeneous fellowship of believers, of all shapes and sizes, whom Christ had called his own at Colossae. Only with them can completeness be found; there can be no path to perfection without them. A powerful dissuasive, indeed, to hasty separation!

b. Let the peace of Christ rule (verse 15)

This exhortation is sometimes misunderstood as a subjective guide to decision-making. Paul is not speaking here of an inner sense of peace as God's gift to those who are in his will: this would make little sense of the second half of the sentence which must control the interpretation, especially if this interpretation is to be kept in line with the context. The Christians, so varied in origins and diverse in character, have been called into 'a single body' (NEB). Probably it is this unique bringing together for which they are to be thankful. Now the rule of Christ is the rule of peace. It is inconceivable that those who share with one another the benefits

13 Lohse, p. 148.

of that great peace-making work of the cross (1:20) should live with any hatred or contempt for each other in their hearts. The Christian congregation should be a realm of peace just because every Christian is totally committed to the rule of peace. When Christ rules in the heart, his peace will rule in the fellowship. It is necessary, however, for Paul to urge this upon the churches in all ages, for Euodia and Syntyche were not the last Christians to find each other impossible.[14]

c. Let the word of Christ dwell in you (verse 16)

As usual in this letter Paul takes every opportunity to stress the centrality and sufficiency of Christ. Elsewhere, in a parallel passage,[15] he can write to the believers about *letting the Holy Spirit fill them*. In Paul's teaching there is never any question of Word and Spirit being separately experienced. The coming of the Word of God in the gospel is the coming of the Spirit, and the coming of the Spirit is the coming of the living and abiding Word of God. Therefore, to enjoy the fullness of the Spirit, a Christian must necessarily be filled with the word of Christ.

A Christian community is happy, therefore, if the word of Christ is *richly*, that is abundantly, available. But it may well be that the visitors looked to other sources by which a 'word' from God might come their way (*cf*. 2.4, 18, 20–22). If so (and how else did they get their authoritative messages?), this must have greatly influenced the teaching they gave, and the type of songs they used for praise: instead of being characterized by the word of Christ, there would be a significant admixture of human doctrines, *i.e.* of religious traditionalism.

For the apostle, therefore, the word of Christ must control all the ministries of the local church. First, there is the *ministry of teaching*. It is intriguing, in view of modern interest in lay ministry, that the work of teaching and admonishing, described in 1:28 as Paul's major function, is here said to be the work of the local congregation, the people (*laos*) of God in one place. How could it be otherwise? A responsibility so vast must be shared. But it will not be carried out *in all wisdom*, that is with sufficient balance and relevance (1:9ff.) if the local congregation itself is not firmly under the word of Christ.

Secondly, there is *the ministry of praise*. Paul likes to pile

---

[14]Phil. 4:2.   [15]Eph. 5:18.

synonyms together,[16] although words that appear synonymous (*e.g.* as here, *teach* and *admonish*) sometimes carry different emphases. In the case of *psalms and hymns and spiritual songs* we shall be wise not to attempt a differentiation, for since the time of Jerome the problem has been debated, and is still unsolved! What is at issue here is the *content* of the young church's hymns. The history of Christian awakening shows that whenever the word of Christ is recovered, it is received with great joy, a joy that can fully express itself only with songs of praise. What the apostle is concerned to see is that these songs are consistent with the word of Christ, or as we are bound to say nowadays, scriptural. A fair test of this is to be found by whether or not they echo a heartfelt spirit of *thankfulness:* genuine Christian praise is not primarily a vehicle for the expression of spiritual aspirations and experiences, so much as a celebration of God's mighty acts in Christ. Lohse has an interesting comment on the normal translation:

> This translation cannot account for the definite article which specifies *charis* as God's bestowal of grace which gives life to the believers. The phrase *en tē chariti* reminds the readers of *sola gratia* (by grace alone) which is the sole basis of existence and creates the realm in which Christian life can exist and develop. This is the reason why God is praised.[17]

Very well. A gospel of grace (1:6) must be echoed by songs of gratitude for grace.

d. Do everything in the name of the Lord Jesus (verse 17)

This general admonition, relevant no doubt in many different situations, must here be understood in its context. The theme is still unity in the congregation. How best can the apostle summarize the way to achieve this?

Notice first, the centrality of Christ, as throughout this sub-section where both 'peace' and 'word' are 'Christ's', when they might equally well have been God's. Absolutely everything that is said and done must be *in the name of the Lord Jesus*. This is the name that unites. We Christians can indeed be one, but only in Christ. The Colossian leaders might therefore set down some such guide for themselves as this: 'All whom Christ has accepted we

---

[16] Lohse, p. 88, for examples.   [17] Lohse, p. 152.

will accept; all who are not satisfied with Christ alone will not be satisfied with us.'

Next, notice that 'whatever we do' takes in our *words*, which must include our teaching, as well as our *deeds*, that is our plans, decisions and activities. There is obvious reference here to the previous verses, even if they cannot exhaust so comprehensive a principle.

Finally, the duty of *giving thanks to God the Father through him*, so often emphasized in this letter, takes us straight back to 1:12.[18] Once again *thankfulness* is Paul's chief prophylactic against the spiritual ills that followed in the wake of the visitors. To promote dissatisfaction, to call in question spiritual attainments, to throw doubts on the completeness of a Christian's salvation—these were their stock-in-trade. Against this Paul called upon the church to recognize the full extent of the treasure they possessed in Jesus Christ their Lord.

The wisdom of this Pauline advice is easily verified. Those Christians who exercise themselves in thanksgiving soon come to possess a much vaster appreciation of the great salvation that is theirs in Christ. And this must also draw them into more appreciative fellowship with all those for whom Christ is the centre of all their hopes.

[18] See pp. 40ff. above.

Colossians 3 : 18–21
The Christian at home

WIVES, be subject to your husbands, as is fitting in the Lord. ¹⁹Husbands, love your wives, and do not be harsh with them. ²⁰Children, obey your parents in everything, for this pleases the Lord. ²¹Fathers, do not provoke your children, lest they become discouraged.

Third in the list of a Christian's relationships are instructions which concern his family life. Whereas in Ephesians the parallel passage is wonderfully enriched with an analogy between Christian marriage and the relation of the church with its Head and Saviour, Christ, in Colossians it is all briefly summarized, with four concise directives. The modern reader, conditioned as he often is to approach Paul warily on the topics of wor   n and marriage, may be wise to read through Ephesians 5 ·   : 4, in order to come to a more just appreciation of th⟋   s high estimate of the Christian household.

These basic rules for the Christian family did not arise *de novo:* contemporary Hellenistic culture already offered such fixed forms of ethical instruction. The neighbours of a Christian couple might well have their own firm ideas as to what was *fitting* and pleasing. The apostolic teaching has not rejected these standards but has christianized them, bringing them all under the rule of Christ. The result is a completely new motivation and inspiration which transforms the 'done thing' into something done for the Lord.

Some critics find these household rules easy to disparage as bourgeois and middle class, and in consequence urge that no attempt should be made to transfer them into our very different

157

world. Such an approach is understandable; what was fitting in Paul's day may appear less suitable today. But a more Christian confidence in apostolic authority will be less confident about the current received wisdom on social relationships, and more ready to suppose that Paul's teaching is a word for our times. In any case, better to start by seeing exactly what this teaching is, and then we shall be in a stronger position to judge whether or not it speaks convincingly to present-day needs.

1. Wives, be subject to your husbands (verse 18)

The apostolic emphasis on *submissiveness* is impressive as well as disconcerting to us moderns: in Ephesians 5:21 Paul prefaces the family and master/slave sections with a kind of 'rule of the road' for social harmony, 'Be subject to one another out of reverence for Christ.' This is therefore to be thought of not as the duty of some, but rather of all. Indeed, so far from being an antiquated barrier to the development of mature human relationships, it is part of the divine order within the Blessed Trinity, where Christ who is equal with the Father[1] is for ever subject to him.[2]

It follows therefore that the rule of life for wives, expressed in this verse, need not be in opposition to the justly famous Galatians 3:28 where the equality of male and female in Christ is celebrated. If the Son is simultaneously equal with the Father and submissive to the Father, then equality and submissiveness can co-exist also in human relationships.

Why then are wives addressed first, surely a slightly curious order if the husband is considered to be leader of the family? This is evidently not the case with wives alone, however, since with every pairing, wives and husbands, children and parents, slaves and masters, the duties of the subordinate party are dealt with first. There seem to be at least two reasons for this. First, and most important, is the easily verifiable fact[3] that the New Testament teaches a 'subordinationist ethic'. This, according to the biblical testimony, is the only way in which human society can work without disintegration.[4] To announce that the modern mind cannot accept this is unhelpful and misleading, since it is evident

---

[1] Jn. 5:18.   [2] 1 Cor. 11:3; 1 Cor. 15:28.
[3] *E.g.* 1 Pet. 2:13 – 3:7; 5:1-5.   [4] See also Jn. 13:12f; Rom. 13:1-7.

that sinful human nature has never liked it, in whatever century.

But just as striking is the indication that, in their respective sections, women and slaves are first addressed, and that with urgency, just because the gospel has already brought them an unique measure of liberation! It is imperative that this wonderful new spiritual freedom should not be misused to the scandalizing of their society and the detriment of the gospel witness. It is precisely because, in Christ, the Christian wife has been set free from the age-old downgrading of her kind in pagan societies, now to enjoy equality with her husband as 'joint heirs of the grace of life'[5] that she must take special care in her behaviour not to cause unnecessary and harmful reactions among her non-Christian neighbours.

It is not simply because certain standards are proper and fitting in the society of their day, however, that Paul commands subjection of the wife to her husband: that might be considered a rather craven surrender to popular but misguided actions, and far from revolutionary as the faith of Christ should be in challenging moral and social attitudes. Surely the apostle is not thus apologetic and accommodating. No! It is his clear teaching that such a way of life is actually fitting *in the Lord*.

Despite this it is still sometimes urged that we ought not to carry this teaching straight into today's world, since Paul is so evidently influenced here, as elsewhere, by his constant concern for the good name of the Christian cause in the particular situation of his own day. In today's world, and in our day, where quite different social patterns of behaviour are normal for women, the question is asked whether a modern apostle would feel forced to call Christian women to something which might even appear to be a step backwards.

No sensitive Christian teacher will want to avoid the force of these objections. The task of applying apostolic principles in today's world demands both an appreciation of the timelessness of New Testament standards, and an awareness of the vast differences we encounter between Paul's age and our own. But in 'translating' Paul for today, the issue at stake is whether we preserve the inner meaning of the original, or effectively abolish it. It is easy, in our impatience, to do the latter.

Much depends upon the meaning of 'subjection', and on the

[5] 1 Pet. 3:7.

context within which this command is set. And straightaway we may emphatically say that it is not a synonym for servile and menial bondage, however often it may have been interpreted in such a way. In the New Testament vocabulary it describes the normal obligations laid upon all men and women as citizens, and upon some men and women as soldiers, young people, workers and wives.[6] It implies that God has so providentially ordered human affairs that a measure of authority must needs be exercised and recognized if human society is to hold together.

Those who might be tempted to be wiser than this will face a hard task to explain away the uncomfortable evidences of human affairs as we experience and observe them, leave alone explaining away the teaching of Peter and Paul! Normally the vacuum created by authorities overthrown (of whatever kind) is quickly filled, so often by a new power more tyrannical than that dreamed of under the old.

What the apostle is teaching, then, is that the family unit is no exception to a universal rule. Even within this small social unit, marked as God intended by love, care and encouragement, there must necessarily be a recognition of a divinely given order. Of course we may disregard this order and refuse this authority. But if this structure is part of the given nature of things as God has made them, we shall do so only at the cost of destroying the thing itself; the family will cease to exist as 'family' in any hitherto accepted sense. We shall then begin to see the 'new family', a secular version (or versions, probably) of the unique divine invention. Christians may be allowed to wonder how effective this substitute will be. If present experience is trustworthy, we may come to see the churches having to offer, through extended families and Christian foster parents, a refuge for the new homeless, that is the deprived children whose parents lived independent lives with no binding concept of the loyalty and love that make a true home possible.

All this is not to say that the woman will always find the sacrificial giving of herself in loyalty to another congenial. But if we are right in seeing this entire ethical section as a sustained exposition of the rule of Christ, the significant truth about a Christian woman's relation to her husband is that it mirrors her commitment to her Lord. What Paul is really explaining is *what it*

[6]Rom. 13:1; Lk. 7:8; 1 Pet. 5:5; 2:18; 3:1.

means to call Christ Lord. In his concept there is no possibility of a married woman's surrender to a heavenly Christ which is not made visible and actual by some submission to an earthly husband. To claim (as I have heard it said) that the discovery of a new loyalty to the Lord made it imperative (apart from exceptional circumstances) to be disloyal to a husband is to enter a pseudo-spiritual world of double-think.

Alas, many husbands do little to deserve the loyalty of a true wife. But Paul has an equally revolutionary word for them.

2. Husbands, love your wives, and do not be harsh with them (verse 19)

Here is some distinctively Christian teaching, to be sure. The Hellenistic world may have known such terms as 'to love' but it did not include them in its rules for the household.[7] And how characteristic of the New Testament to *command* love![8]

Notice also that Paul urges mutual responsibilities upon husband and wife: it is not all one-sided. Indeed her side is hardly possible without his, and vice versa. The two imperatives ought not to be isolated, and then one of them emphasized without thought for its dependence on the other. How natural to love a loyal wife! And who would not want to remain loyal to a truly loving husband?

Sadly, we easily deceive ourselves in these matters, and men more readily than women. To say 'I love you' has always been conspicuously easy.[9] It is again characteristic of the New Testament to give to Christians, in this case husbands, a practical test by which each may be able to recognize the genuineness or otherwise of his devotion to his spouse. *Do not be harsh* (lit. embittered) *with them* is a salutary reminder that bitterness easily creeps into human dealings and then justifies itself so as to become even more deeply entrenched. A wife can disappoint a man's hopes and ambitions, failing to live up to his unrealistic ideals for her (which are often an unconscious compensation for his own inadequacies). Tiredness and ill-temper mean that such feelings of disappointment quickly find expression in harsh words.

How horrifyingly easy it is for us to destroy human

---

[7] Lohse, p. 158, note 28.   [8] *E.g.* 2 John 6.   [9] 1 John 3 : 18; 4 : 20.

relationships, even the closest and dearest. It is in making ourselves into the lord we serve that others are destroyed by us: because they have not served us as we think we deserve, we seek vengeance. Quite opposite is the Christian way as exemplified in Ephesians 5:25ff.: such creative constructiveness *is* love. It makes a person what they would not otherwise become.

As before, the context is decisive for our interpretation. The rule of Christ demands that a man serve his wife as the evidence that he is serving Christ. So once again we have, worked out in daily life, what it means to make Christ Lord.

3. Children, obey your parents (verse 20)

Next, Paul turns to the relationship of parents and children. Once more it is daring to summarize complex relations in such short compass, and as before the controlling theme is the rule of Christ. So the underlying question is, How can a Christian child express his or her desire to serve the Lord Jesus?

The instruction is to *obey your parents in everything, for this pleases the Lord*. Here obedience is an appropriate illustration of what submissiveness means. Without such obedience, whether willing or not, mothers and fathers cannot exercise the privileges of parenthood. The less the obedience they receive, the less the happiness and encouragement they can give. In other words the apostolic injunction is not arbitrary; without it no constructive relationship can be secured. Disobedient children are one of the more disagreeable and alarming signs of decay in a Christian culture. It means that biblical sanity is on the way out, and it is particularly distressing when propagated in the name of kindness and progress. No wonder that sensible Dr Spock had second thoughts!

The phrase *in everything* can raise difficulties. But is it not characteristic of Paul to give a basic rule for the churches without qualification,[10] leaving it to experience and spiritual wisdom to discover the inevitable limitations of such rules?[11] Sometimes he qualifies one of his own 'rules for all the churches'.[12] But we are wise to acknowledge the force of Paul's all-embracing language, and not to jump too eagerly to the task of

[10] *E.g.* Rom. 13:1.   [11] *E.g.* Acts 4:19-20.
[12] 1 Cor. 7:17-24, esp. verse 21: though see C. K. Barrett, *The First Epistle to the Corinthians*, pp. 170f.

dismantling it by finding exceptions. In any case, to do something evidently displeasing to the Lord at the command of parents would hardly be pleasing to the Lord: so the incentive shrewdly balances the imperative.

Once again we may well see in Paul's language, *for this pleases*, a 'recognized social value' of the day.[13] Yet we ought not to conclude from this that Paul happily fits in with prevalent cultural attitudes, contenting himself with sanctifying such standards by tacking on '*the Lord*'. It would be hard to find any practical family instruction more rooted in every part of Holy Scripture than the importance of children's obedience to their parents. In the Bible stories spoilt children rarely learn to serve God.[14] And surely this gets us to the heart of the matter; if there are no spoilt children in God's family, how painful will be the lot of the Christian disciple who, long before conversion perhaps, was foolishly indulged at home![15] Home, not church, is the place where this lesson is to be learned, a lesson in which lie nearly all the possibilities, in any life of Christian service, for future usefulness and honour.[16]

As always, Paul shows that there is another side to every relationship. It is not the case that all the rights are on one side, and all the duties on the other. History and literature show how often children have received little but curses, while nothing has been asked from them but cringing servility. In such a situation the rule of Christ is as revolutionary as ever.

4. Fathers, do not provoke your children (verse 21)

Those commentators who ask why mothers are not included here might also ask whether mothers are as likely to need this instruction. It is problem fathers who are more likely to be the cause of problem children. What is evil here is the destructive nature of such provocations as endless criticism and harsh punishments. To encourage a person is creative; it is to stir him to do and be what otherwise would never have been achieved (see the only other occurrence of this word in the New Testament, 2 Cor. 9:2). The result of the irritable parent is to produce 'discouraged' children in the sense that they are fearful and timid,

---

[13] Lohse, p. 159, note 35, quoting the Dibelius–Greeven commentary *An Die Kolosser, Epheser, an Philemon* (*HNT* 12, Tübingen, 1953).

[14] *E.g.* 1 Ki. 1:6; was this true of Absalom too?

[15] Heb. 12:3–11, esp. verse 11.　　[16] Heb. 12:9.

shy and lacking in normal self-confidence. It is no use such a father bemoaning the inability of his children to be strong and self-reliant like himself, since he has used his strength to crush and undermine them.

It is now possible to look back on this section and try to estimate its continuing significance. Certainly it brilliantly reveals the secret of happy families, and as splendidly shows how those who might remain weak become strong. Is it too much to say that here is laid down an important foundation for a healthy society? Yet none of this is thought of as possible without the rule of Christ. The strong do not use their strength for the benefit of those who cannot compel them unless mastered by the Lord of love. Nor does anyone willingly yield allegiance to another, since we are all self-willed, unless constrained by love, and, best of all, love for the Lord. Can we improve on this description of mutual dependence in the family? Can we regard it lightly and expect Christian family life to survive?

Colossians 3:22 – 4:1
The Christian at work

SLAVES, obey in everything those who are your earthly masters, not with eyeservice, as men-pleasers, but in singleness of heart, fearing the Lord. [23]Whatever your task, work heartily, as serving the Lord and not men, [24]knowing that from the Lord you will receive the inheritance as your reward; you are serving the Lord Christ. [25]For the wrongdoer will be paid back for the wrong he has done, and there is no partiality.

[4:1]Masters, treat your slaves justly and fairly, knowing that you also have a Master in heaven.

The good news of a Christ who came to set us free[1] is seldom far from Paul's mind as he writes his Colossian letter. At the start he had explained that 'deliverance for the captive' was an essential part of the meaning and experience of forgiveness (1:13, 14). And as we know, it was because the visitors had taken hold of this exciting concept of spiritual freedom, and presented it in an exaggerated (and therefore even more exciting) and potentially harmful way, that the apostle was alert to protect the gospel from misunderstanding and the Colossian Christians from misguided action in the pursuit of a fuller 'liberty'.

You cannot preach freedom from the old inequalities as Paul did (*e.g.* 'There is neither Jew nor Greek, there is neither slave nor free, there is neither male nor female; for you are all one in Christ Jesus'),[2] without being asked how in practice this works out in a society where these inequalities continue unchanged. If it seemed necessary to say a word to Christian wives and husbands lest their

---

[1] *Cf.* Lk. 4:18.   [2] Gal. 3:28; *cf.* Col. 3:11.

newfound 'freedom in Christ' drive a wedge between them, and between them and their neighbours (thereby discrediting the notion of spiritual liberty), how much more urgent to say something to slaves and masters! It must have been bewildering at times for both sides, and threatening too, not only for those within the little Christian communities, but also for those who anxiously looked on, deeply disturbed at what seemed likely to overthrow the stability of their social order.

The cause of liberation for the oppressed appeals to us today as deeply, and probably more widely, than at any time in history. Understandably, in some parts of the world there is a demand for 'liberation theology'. Against this background even Christian readers of Paul have expressed feelings ranging from uncertainty through embarrassment to downright disappointment that the apostle appears so content with the status quo, and so apparently unwilling to call for some measure of social change. Even the haste with which his defenders point out the sheer impossibility, if not absurdity, of attempting to alter the economic base of a vast empire,[3] or point with some justification to the eventual triumph of the gospel in the abolition of slavery; even this haste only serves to show that they are conscious of the weight of the attack.

Of course Paul has other things to say on this sensitive topic apart from this brief paragraph of instruction before us: notably there is his letter to Philemon which vividly preserves for us some early evidence of the impact of the gospel on the slave/master relationship, and leaves us very much aware that a new spirit was being let loose in Roman society which could not be contained in the old forms. We study this later, but for the moment, with this Colossian section before us, it is wise once again to pay the apostle the compliment of listening to what he actually has to say.

At first glance it seems that, far from removing the yoke of slavery, Paul has fastened it more firmly than ever. Christian slaves are told to *obey in everything those who are your earthly masters*. Can this really mean to place them on the level of childhood for ever, with its inevitable limitations (note the parallel between verse 20 and verse 22a), and yet without that great hope of childhood, that one day adult estate will be attained?

A closer look, however, tells quite another story; it reveals the

[3] As Lohse says, to ask Paul to command the freeing of slaves is to be guilty of unhistorical thinking; p. 162, note 73.

development of a remarkable insight that Paul would share with the believing slaves. He wishes them to understand that, in a very real sense, *they are now not serving men at all*. This is explicit in verse 23; in their work they are 'serving the Lord, and *not men*'. This negative statement is supported by the other negative of verse 22, *not with eyeservice, as men-pleasers*: together they clear the way for the positive teaching that everything the slave now does is part of his new work for the Lord. From his miserable servitude he has been rescued, at a stroke, to become a full-time servant of Christ.

With this clue in our hands we can now appreciate the force of each succeeding verse, setting it out in this way.

1. The slave is set free from 'men-pleasing'

The unique word 'eyeservice' means either work that is done because the boss has his eye upon one or that which is done with an eye to catch his attention. In other words it is all a matter of external appearances. The slave does only that which is necessary to attract favour or escape punishment. He does nothing more—why should he?—than what is required to satisfy his overseer, and remain, as we would say, 'in his good books'. This universal practice soon becomes a fine art; the appearance of obedience is there, but the reality is very different. As all human experience verifies, whether the boss is a first-century slave-master or an impersonal twentieth-century corporation, much time and thought is then taken up in seeing how personal ends can be served, while yet doing just sufficient to avoid the employer's wrath.

But now, from servility and all these prevarications the Christian is delivered. And with what result? He is set free—astonishing thought—to do everything his master asks of him! All prudential considerations and ulterior motives can be set aside, and every wish carried out, not to please or placate a man who cannot be denied, but as the only way in which the rule of Christ can be acknowledged. To call Christ Lord is to fear to displease him: yet that godly fear sooner or later sets one free from lesser and unworthy fears. While his pagan comrade *might* 'obey in everything' his earthly master, for fear of him, the Christian slave can now actually bring himself to 'obey in everything' that same master, but for wholly different reasons.

167

2. The slave is set free to work wholeheartedly

The transformation described in verse 22 is very great; but can such new obedience be rendered willingly and with the whole heart? This is a serious question which deserves and receives more than a glib answer. If it were a matter of being a slave of another person however kind and fair, then while duty might be done willingly enough in the name of the Lord Jesus (as verse 17 commands), it could not be done 'from the soul' (as it is described in the Greek of Eph. 6:6). For in the depths of our being we know that we were not meant to be the property of another; the heart cries out against such unnatural bondage. No, we can give the allegiance of our souls only to the Lord;[4] and no Christian can give this 'worship' to any other power but God.

Negatively there is guidance here as to what a Christian slave cannot be, whatever law and custom demand, namely the possession of another human being. But paradoxically, as it may seem at first, this assurance of individual worth and dignity opens the way to a wholehearted service of the slave's master (whether worthy or not). And this is so because it now recognized that, in Christ, the slave's worth is such that any task he undertakes for his master, however menial, is fit to be part of his service of the Lord of glory. It is not only that he can do this work (of all works) as though Christ were doing it (so verse 17); he can do it knowing that it is done *for* Christ, and that he (of all masters) is willing to receive it (so verse 23).

3. The slave is set free from work without proper reward

Though verse 24 is part of the reasoning that began in the previous verse, it is well to consider it separately, and not to overlook its link with verse 25. Once more the Christian slave is reminded solemnly that he is, in truth, serving the Lord Christ. As a result he can know for sure that while exploitation may be his earthly lot (the master would pay no wages), he will yet receive a proper recompense from his heavenly Master. And this cuts both ways. Applied to the slave, verse 25 is a sharp reminder that previous habits of poor service would be poorly recompensed by this new master who is strictly fair and impartial, and who does not, as human masters will do, unjustly favour the oppressed

[4]Mk. 12:30.

simply because they have never been favoured before—a healthy insight into the lack of sentimentalism in the kingdom of Christ.

But is there nothing in verse 25 for the earthly masters? It is true that they are not formally addressed until the next verse (4:1), but it is difficult to avoid the feeling that Paul saw the validity of verse 25 as having application just as clearly to them: probably the very enunciation of the principle led his mind to consider the responsibilities of such slave owners. For who was the greater wrongdoer, the slave who held back his labour as far as circumstances permitted, or the master who held back a proper reward for those labours, because circumstances did permit?

It is of course a wholly new idea that the master should be regarded as having any binding responsibilities towards his slaves: no doubt where Paul's teaching was known it caused much indignation in the places where slave-owners met together. Such notions could only be considered reckless and impertinent. But no doubt there were some slave-owners who would listen (there were people like Philemon in the earliest congregations), and those who became Christians would come to acknowledge that this new relationship to their heavenly Lord must inevitably control *all* their activities, even in handling their slaves.

This new rule of Christ was, above all, just and fair (4:1). That which Christ had shown in his dealings with them, they in turn must demonstrate to their servants. The extraordinary nature of this quiet command can be appreciated only by recalling the plight of the slave, without recourse to justice and equity in any form. Yet here it is said that he must be given what he cannot claim, and what no-one would think of claiming for him. It may well be, in the social conditions of the times, that this brief command, *Treat your slaves justly and fairly*, was even harder to carry out than anything asked of the slaves, possibly involving their owners in a measure of social ostracism, quite apart from the financial problems. But of this we shall hear more in Philemon.

Looking back over the whole section we are now in a position to consider whether Paul's teaching opens him to legitimate criticisms for failing to make a more effective protest against the iniquities of slavery, or whether we are compelled to say that he had found a more excellent way. One benefit of this close study is that we can begin to see emerging from this teaching *Paul's priorities*.

First, the apostle's paramount concern is not man's relationships with his fellows, but everyone's relationship with God. Paul does not attempt to resolve these human problems between slave and master horizontally. It is clear that he assumes that it is only by learning to serve the Lord Christ that each can begin to come to proper terms with the other. For what is it that he wants each to know? Is it not that both have a Lord in heaven (see 'knowing' in 3:24 and 4:1)? This can never be the world's way of tackling social and industrial relationships; but the church has no commission to preach the kingdom of God without talking about the King (notice how the Lord is mentioned four times in these four verses). Furthermore Paul is able boldly to mention heavenly rewards and sanctions, an example we now fear to follow (in the face of Marxist scorn), with an inevitable, if surprising, loss of credibility.

It is no use disparaging this approach as pietistic and over-individualistic, unless we can see results like Paul's. For notice how the Christian slave is now taken up, not with his own needs, but with his master's—does *he* get the labour he has the right to expect? Notice too how the master, when similarly reorientated to Christ, is now taken up, not with his own needs but with those of his slaves—do *they* get the reward they have a right to enjoy? Is not this an eminently desirable revolution in human attitudes? But by what human power or sociological expertise can it be accomplished?

Secondly, the apostle's great concern is with the present rather than the future. This letter is addressed to the members of a church, not to the leaders of society. It is meant to help the believers with their *present* problems and rescue them from their *present* miseries and dangers. It would bring slaves yet more misery if Paul were to tell them to revolt, nor would it be any comfort to think that apostolic protests against social evils might change things in a future too far off to benefit any of them. The glory of the gospel is that it has something to give in the worst situations we experience. Just there and then it is possible to live victoriously. Paul's message brought happiness and fulfilment into the here and now. The purpose of Paul's ministry was to set people free in Christ now, and it is doubtful whether he had any visionary dreams of a time coming when slavery would be abolished. When that happened, however, it was the weapons he forged that won the victory. What a benefactor he was!

Colossians 4:2-6
The Christian and the outsider

CONTINUE steadfastly in prayer, being watchful in it with thanksgiving; ³and pray for us also, that God may open to us a door for the word, to declare the mystery of Christ, on account of which I am in prison, ⁴that I may make it clear, as I ought to speak. ⁵Conduct yourselves wisely toward outsiders, making the most of the time. ⁶Let your speech always be gracious, seasoned with salt, so that you may know how you ought to answer every one.

The final section descriptive of life under the rule of Christ turns the believers' attention outwards in order that they might recognize their responsibilities to make the truth of the gospel known to those outside the Christian community. It is not 'a loose sequence of a few additional admonitions' (Lohse), but a tightly constructed section giving basic outlines of Christian duty to spread the Word. It answers realistically the question, What can an ordinary group of believing people do to make sure that outsiders *hear* of Christ? It assumes that the church is committed by lip as well as by life to witness to the saving message, while accepting that comparatively few individual Christians are called to preach.

The balance and thrust of the section may be conveyed by the following division.

1. Speaking to God about people (verses 2–4)
2. Speaking to people about God (verses 5–6)

1. Speaking to God about people (verses 2–4)

Effective evangelism begins with persevering prayer. Both Paul

171

and Epaphras are conspicuous examples to the Colossian flock in this work where Christian leadership so often fails (1:9 and 4:12). To *continue steadfastly* is to persevere, and to persevere is to busy oneself with the task in hand, rather like that energetic little widow who gave her local magistrate no rest.[1] A characteristic mark of the earliest Christians is their devotion to intercessory prayer.[2] Was it that the visitors laid small stress on this that Paul must emphasize so clear a duty? More likely the Colossians had grown sleepy, if our own experience is any guide: and such failure to 'watch and pray'[3] had made them poor guardians when the testing crisis came. It is in a prayerless church that the enemy can best do his work of disruption.

The emphasis on *thanksgiving* is, as we now know, a characteristic of this letter, sufficiently marked for comment. Here it is the best and necessary companion of the prayer that perseveres. Prayer can no more exist without praise than true praise without prayer: the one fuels the other.

But for what are they particularly to pray? Paul's request for their prayers is surely not a matter of returning like for like in consideration of his prayers for them. No, he asks their prayers because of his known commission to preach. This is God's calling for him, and a prison sentence cannot countermand the divine orders. Significantly, he does not ask them to pray that God would open the doors of the prison for his release, though he is no superman without feeling for his condition (note the final appeal for sympathy concerning his fetters, verse 18). Those doors might well open if only he would stop his preaching, for it is *on account of* this that he suffers. But, victoriously, the apostle asks for yet another 'open door', or God-given opportunity,[4] so that he may *declare the mystery of Christ*. Nowhere else does Paul use 'to declare' to describe his preaching.[5] Here it seems that to describe Christian ministry as a declaration of something previously hidden is to make Christian preaching a part of the process of revelation. This startling apostolic concept is in need of rediscovery today. The revelation of God in Christ has already been given in history, and written in Scripture. But it must also be spoken by God's servants if people's minds are to be opened to the truth. In this sense every Christian sermon should be an 'eye-

---

[1] Lk. 18:1–8.   [2] Acts 1:14; 2:42; 6:4, *etc.*   [3] Mt. 26:41.
[4] 1 Cor. 16:9; 2 Cor. 2:12.   [5] Lohse, p. 165.

opener' (Acts 26:18). It is by human speech that divine truth is made *clear, i.e.* made known. And remember, this had been the actual experience of the Colossians who had come to learn and understand the truth through the preaching of Epaphras (1:5-7).

It is of great interest that the first duty of the Christians in Colossae was to open their mouths in prayer for the preachers of the gospel whom God had evidently called to this work. It was not, by inference, their first duty themselves to preach. The fresh and necessary awakening of the churches today to the concept of 'every-member ministry', and the mobilization of all Christians to take the gospel to all the world, should not be allowed to tone down this truth. Those who preach among the churches without a gift or call from God will not greatly advance the cause of truth: even more certainly, those believers who mistakenly feel called to 'preach' in the home and at work, indeed among all the normal affairs of life, will hardly win a hearing for their Lord. They are likely to face closing doors rather than opening ones, and, if not sent to prison, may land up in social isolation.

But surely, someone protests, the lips of Christians are not meant to be sealed. If I believe, must I not speak?[6] To this, verses 5 and 6 give a satisfying reply.

2. Speaking to people about God (verses 5-6)

Yes, the Christian does have the responsibility of 'speaking to people about God'. Just as there is an 'ought' about the apostle's speaking, so there is an 'ought' about theirs. But a comparison between the two final phrases in each half of the section shows a difference in emphasis that is of some significance. They are to pray for the apostle that he might make the gospel known as he *ought to speak.* He in turn gives them sound advice so that they may know how they *ought to answer* everyone.

We may describe this difference by saying that while the apostle looks for many opportunities for *direct* evangelism and teaching, the typical Christian in Colossae is to look for many opportunities for *responsive* evangelism.

If this distinction is a correct one, it immediately commends itself by its sanity and realism. Harm can be done by sincere believing people who feel compelled to preach and testify to those

[6] 2 Cor. 4:13.

with whom they mix in shop or office. Rightly aware of the importance of their message, the sad ignorance of many of their neighbours, and the urgency of the times, they plunge in bravely (whatever the temperature!). But direct assault on entrenched apathy (to change the metaphor) is seldom successful and can never be carried out by normally sensitive people without great cost to nerve and confidence. Alas, one consequence of failure in such verbal witnessing is a discouragement sufficiently severe at times to lead to disengagement from this part of the battle altogether.

Now Paul's advice to the Christians is not along the lines of possessing oneself of better techniques with which to approach people. Rather he turns the problem right around so that the Christians can see their responsibilities in a much more promising light. Their privilege, simply put, is to *answer everyone*. That is to say they are to respond to the questions of others rather than initiate conversations on leading topics; they are to *accept* openings rather than *make* them.

This is, emphatically, not to sound the retreat. Paul evidently believes that opportunities for response and explanation are to be found everywhere, for everyone is looking to discover answers about life and its meaning. And Paul evidently thinks that believing Christians should be found everywhere too, ready to take up these frequent opportunities.

It is obvious what strain this removes from conscientious Christians. The pressure to raise certain topics and reach certain people can make it difficult to live or talk normally. In any case, we go to the office to work, not to evangelize. But by being ready and willing to respond the way is opened to a more serene, and successful, approach to each day's opportunities. It opens the way, too, for a greater dependence on God's leading as well as for a more relevant and sensitive witness, suited to each individual. And remember, when the outsider has chosen the time and the place and the subject, how wonderfully free is the Christian to 'open his mouth' and tell 'the good news of Jesus'.[7]

The qualities that will make for effectiveness in 'answering everyone' are well chosen and nicely balanced. The Christian must *conduct himself wisely toward outsiders*, but wisdom is not to be

[7] Acts 8:35, where although Philip was a full-time evangelist, his dealings with the distinguished Ethiopian are a model of 'responsive evangelism'.

used as an excuse for over much caution. He is to *make the most of the time* available, and time is always short. It is never easy to hold these two aspects together. The new convert, typically, is urgent, but can lack tact and discretion. The older Christian has the wisdom of experience, but often lacks boldness and importunity. Given this right balance between zeal and tact in conduct, there is also a balance in speech to be learned. This Christian speaking must *always be gracious*, especially when answers provoke argument.[8] But gracious words can be insipid and dull, so the apostle asks for some seasoning as well. It is too much to equate *salt* with wit, but it is not too much to say that our answers should compel interest and attention. Piquancy is an important characteristic of the speech that wins people.

Perhaps the abiding impression left by this most practical section is that there is never a time, according to Paul, when our responsibilities to the *outsider* (verse 5) can be out of mind. Always we must be praying that opportunities for the gospel to be preached to them will be given by God. Always we must gladly take those opportunities, however unpropitious our circumstances. Always we must use the fleeting moments for Christian response when people give us opportunities. And always, however far off in understanding the questioner may be, we must seek the wisdom and grace to answer with words that will awaken his appetite for the things of Christ.

At the end of the five sections of 'applied Christianity' (beginning at 3:1), it may be of interest to notice their order and sequence. Put together they combine to show an all-round consistency in Christian living. But no doubt there are other lessons, more or less obvious, to be learned. For example, the close connection between the believer's relationships to Christ and the local church is plain—you cannot properly have one without the other—yet the two relationships are by no means identical, and are described separately. And is it not impossible to miss what is implicit in the fact that of all the sections, that on the verbal expression of our faith is put last? For without the backing of a genuine Christian life, reaching beyond church to home and work, our words of witness will lack the ring of truth.

[8] *Cf.* 2 Tim. 2:24-25.

Colossians 4:7–18
Final greetings and instructions

*T*YCHICUS *will tell you all about my affairs; he is a beloved brother and faithful minister and fellow servant in the Lord.* [8]*I have sent him to you for this very purpose, that you may know how we are and that he may encourage your hearts,* [9]*and with him Onesimus, the faithful and beloved brother, who is one of yourselves. They will tell you of everything that has taken place here.*

[10]*Aristarchus my fellow prisoner greets you, and Mark the cousin of Barnabas (concerning whom you have received instructions—if he comes to you, receive him),* [11]*and Jesus who is called Justus. These are the only men of the circumcision among my fellow workers for the kingdom of God, and they have been a comfort to me.* [12]*Epaphras, who is one of yourselves, a servant of Christ Jesus, greets you, always remembering you earnestly in his prayers, that you may stand mature and fully assured in all the will of God.* [13]*For I bear him witness that he has worked hard for you and for those in Laodicea and Hierapolis.* [14]*Luke the beloved physician and Demas greet you.* [15]*Give my greetings to the brethren at Laodicea, and to Nympha and the church in her house.* [16]*And when this letter has been read among you, have it read also in the church of the Laodiceans; and see that you read also the letter from Laodicea.* [17]*And say to Archippus, 'See that you fulfil the ministry which you have received in the Lord.'*

[18]*I, Paul, write this greeting with my own hand. Remember my fetters. Grace be with you.*

A comparison with Paul's other letters shows that the Colossian epilogue is unusually rich in personal messages and greetings.

Only the conclusion of the Roman epistle can be compared with it.

Its purpose is self-evidently to strengthen the apostle's ties with the Christian people in Colossae as well as with the churches in the neighbourhood (15-16). Paul clearly believes that his imprisonment is not dangerous for himself alone; it involves real perils for the churches from which he is forcibly separated. While he is unavoidably absent, others are free to step in and cause mischief.[1] And in fact this is what has happened in the churches of the Lycus valley.

Underlying the entire Colossian letter is this desire of Paul's that the closest possible links between himself and these churches should be forged. He wants them to realize how closely he is concerned for them, and how intimately he feels himself to be with them in their problems (cf. 2:1-5).

It is for these reasons that he quietly emphasizes that, because of what he has heard, he is not ignorant of the kind of people they are; for has he not close personal knowledge of people such as Onesimus and Epaphras of whom it can be said 'he is *one of yourselves*' (verses 9, 12)?

Paul knows about their affairs (verses 15-17), and wants them to know about his (verses 7-9). He well knows that without frequent news of one another no relationship can flourish. He has no desire to be a general so far removed from the front lines that confidence withers and dies. He sees that good communications are the essence of influence, and acts accordingly.

Nor does the apostle give any impression to them that his authority is in temporary abeyance because of his imprisonment. He sends Tychicus and Onesimus on their mission (verses 7-9); he reinforces instructions about Mark (verse 10): he requires that his letters be circulated to other churches (verse 16), and he sends an urgent and public message to Archippus. No apostle emeritus here!

Perhaps most interesting of all are the indications that abound in this epilogue of the sort of person Paul was.

He had a great capacity for people. It was not just that he remembered their names; Romans 16:1-15 is sufficient proof of this. He also cared deeply for many of them. Was it partly at least because he had no family of his own that he could give himself so unstintingly to the Lord's family? At any rate, one reason why he

[1] *Cf.* Acts 20:29.

was loved so greatly is that he was a man who greatly loved.[2]

He had a great capacity for sharing his ministry. Tychicus is his *fellow servant*, Aristarchus his *fellow prisoner* and also, with Mark and Justus, one of his *fellow workers*. It is one thing to be glad that other men should share the pain of his imprisonment; but it is quite another to be willing that they should share the privileges of a great ministry. Paul brought other qualified and mature believers into a genuine partnership with himself. In this the older churches of the West, at least, have still largely to learn from him.

He had a great capacity for supporting his lieutenants. None ever worked for a more appreciative leader than did the helpers of Paul. We have already observed his emphatic public approval of Epaphras (12–13; *cf.* 1:7). But whether it was friends who apparently had risked their necks for him on one occasion,[3] or his personal doctor (verse 14), their efforts are remarked and noticed with genuine gratitude.[4]

It is of interest to see what Paul appreciated, and no surprise to find faithfulness, *i.e.* loyalty, and hard work, high on his list (7, 9, 11, 13; again *cf.* Rom. 16:6, 12).

He had a great capacity for singlemindedness. What a man Paul is for never letting up! He wrote this letter to the Colossians with the need of their loyalty in mind (1:2). And loyalty is the very heart of his message to them (2:6, 7). So it is surely significant that while loyalty is unremarked in Romans 16, it is pointedly mentioned in this letter (1:7) and in this epilogue (7, 9), otherwise only in the parallel passages in Ephesians (1:1; 6:12).

But still more telling is the fact that the apostle will not allow his readers to escape the basic appeal of his letter, even in this informal epilogue. The thorough-going refutation of the pseudo-spiritual fullness offered by the visitors is over. Now it is of positive Christian experience that he would speak. The false fullness went hand in hand with immaturity (as at Corinth, *e.g.* 1 Cor. 4:8), but he echoes the desire of their good friend Epaphras for them, that they should be *mature*, and be 'filled with everything that is God's will' (Lohse's translation)[5] Perhaps, too, the exhortation to Archippus was along these lines, though no

---

[2] Verses 7, 9, 14, and compare Rom. 16:5, 8, 9, 12.   [3] Rom. 16:4.
[4] *Cf.* Rom. 16:2.
[5] See Lohse, p. 173, for the justification of this difference from RSV.

certainty about this man's ministry is possible. At all events he is to be able to show a 'completed' ministry if and when the apostle comes.[6]

So, as Paul says farewell to us, we need remember his fetters no more, for they have long since rusted away. But we do remember his encouragement to us, that in Christ Jesus we may enjoy fullness of life and freedom, and his exhortation to us to fulfil any ministry that we may have received while there is time.

[6] Phm. 2, 22.

The letter to Philemon

Philemon 1–25
From slavery to freedom

*P*AUL, *a prisoner for Christ Jesus, and Timothy our brother,*
   To Philemon our beloved fellow worker ²*and Apphia our
sister and Archippus our fellow soldier, and the church in your
house:*

³*Grace to you and peace from God our Father and the Lord Jesus
Christ.*

⁴*I thank my God always when I remember you in my prayers,*
⁵*because I hear of your love and of the faith which you have toward
the Lord Jesus and all the saints,* ⁶*and I pray that the sharing of
your faith may promote the knowledge of all the good that is ours
in Christ.* ⁷*For I have derived much joy and comfort from your
love, my brother, because the hearts of the saints have been
refreshed through you.*

⁸*Accordingly, though I am bold enough in Christ to command
you to do what is required,* ⁹*yet for love's sake I prefer to appeal to
you—I, Paul, an ambassador and now a prisoner also for Christ
Jesus—*¹⁰*I appeal to you for my child, Onesimus, whose father I
have become in my imprisonment.* ¹¹*(Formerly he was useless to
you, but now he is indeed useful to you and to me.)* ¹²*I am sending
him back to you, sending my very heart.* ¹³*I would have been glad
to keep him with me, in order that he might serve me on your
behalf during my imprisonment for the gospel;* ¹⁴*but I preferred
to do nothing without your consent in order that your goodness
might not be by compulsion but of your own free will.*

¹⁵*Perhaps this is why he was parted from you for a while, that
you might have him back for ever,* ¹⁶*no longer as a slave but more
than a slave, as a beloved brother, especially to me but how much
more to you, both in the flesh and in the Lord.* ¹⁷*So if you consider*

me your partner, receive him as you would receive me. [18]*If he has wronged you at all, or owes you anything, charge that to my account.* [19]*I, Paul, write this with my own hand, I will repay it—to say nothing of your owing me even your own self.* [20]*Yes, brother, I want some benefit from you in the Lord. Refresh my heart in Christ.*

[21]*Confident of your obedience, I write to you, knowing that you will do even more than I say.* [22]*At the same time, prepare a guest room for me, for I am hoping through your prayers to be granted to you.*

[23]*Epaphras, my fellow prisoner in Christ Jesus, sends greetings to you,* [24]*and so do Mark, Aristarchus, Demas, and Luke, my fellow workers.*

[25]*The grace of the Lord Jesus Christ be with your spirit.*

Paul's letter to Philemon is one of the special treasures of the New Testament. It is of unique interest to us as the only surviving example, from the apostle's no doubt vast correspondence, of a letter to an individual friend and convert. Yet the envelope is by no means marked 'personal and private'. While the 'you's' and 'yours' of verses 4 to 21 are singular and refer to Philemon—for it is his attitude and decisions about which Paul is chiefly concerned—the 'you's' and 'yours' of the greeting (verse 3) and conclusion (verses 22–25) are plural. So it is evidently an open letter, to be received and read by the church in Philemon's house as well. The significance of this shared responsibility will become apparent later.

Although the situation has been read differently,[1] there seems no solid ground for abandoning the traditional interpretation.

Philemon was a well-to-do man, very likely with a considerable household. Was it business interests that originally led him to Ephesus, and so within Paul's sphere of influence? Certainly he owed his own faith in Christ to the apostle's ministry (verse 19), and with so many others had become, in consequence, a willing partner in the great enterprises of the gospel. Back at home, his house became the meeting place of a Christian congregation (verse 2). And if, as is sometimes suggested, Apphia was his wife,

---

[1]John Knox, *Philemon Among the Letters of Paul: A New View of its Place and Importance* (Chicago Press, 1935); *cf.* John Knox, *Philemon (The Interpreter's Bible,* Abingdon, 1955).

and Archippus their son, then we have a pleasant picture of a family united in this Christian service, Apphia with her natural role as hostess to these 'fellowship groups', and Archippus just beginning to use the spiritual gifts and ministry that he had evidently received for the good of the churches, in Laodicea as well as in Colossae.[2]

Altogether it sounds a good house for any believer to know: little wonder that the apostle dreamed of release from the galling fetters of Rome, and the prospect of that guest room with the joy of renewed fellowship with his old friend (verse 22).

Onesimus had been one of Philemon's slaves. Always an unsatisfactory servant (verse 11), he may have further injured his master by robbing him (verse 18) before absconding in a bid for freedom. Yet the only 'freedom' he could hope to enjoy in such a situation was a wretched thing, an existence lived in constant dread of discovery and always near to starvation, shifting as best he could among the dregs of a great city. Was it desperation, therefore, that drove Onesimus to seek out the confined apostle? Had he heard his master speak with awe and affection of the great Christian leader? Whatever the circumstances, it makes a dramatic scene, even in Paul's adventurous life, as the fugitive slave anxiously finds his way to the man who was to become his spiritual father and benefactor (verse 10).

But now it is time for him to return to Colossae. No doubt Onesimus would willingly have remained in Rome serving the apostle's needs, but the duty laid upon him by his new discovery of Christ was clear. He must go back to the master he has wronged and give himself up. Easy to say, but not to do, for Onesimus had been guilty of one of the most serious offences known to ancient law. He could expect only great severity, possibly death itself.[3]

But Onesimus is comforted by two factors—the reassuring presence of a Christian companion, Tychicus, a man of some standing among the churches;[4] and a knowledge of the letter they are carrying with them from the apostle to Philemon. And there is a third reason for hope. Like everybody else the returning slave has cause to know not only from what was widely reported

[2] Col. 4:16-17.
[3] The fear of slave-risings was so great that often extreme and savage vengeance would be meted out, something not unfamiliar in the modern world when minorities repress majorities.
[4] Col. 4·7-9.

(verses 4–7), but from past experience, of the benevolence and kindness of his master.

We will open this delightful letter, then, and consider its contents. It will not be easy for us to treat it lightly, as apparently happened among some of the earliest Christian churches,[5] since for us the relation of the gospel of Christ to social issues, not least those to do with man's exploitation of man, are at present matters of acute concern and frequent debate.

It may be that our danger is nearer to those who, in more recent generations, have thought to enlist Paul on their side either as spiritual reactionaries or as revolutionaries. When Christian people have sought to justify domestic slavery on the grounds that Paul does not here seek the overthrow of the accepted (and, economically, almost necessary) social order of his day, this letter is grievously ill-used. Especially must this be the case when such voices arise from a culture which, because it is impregnated with Christian truth, supported by Christian consciences, and in large measure committed to Christian standards, is very different from Paul's day.

On the other hand, to read this letter in the hope of finding apostolic protests against this most radical evil in the ancient world is a frankly disappointing exercise. It is not that Paul lacks the necessary commitment or compassion, for genuine concern is evident in every phrase. It is rather that this concern is directed simply to one particular incident and to one small group of people. It is because of this narrowness of scope that certain early writers spoke of the letter's 'triviality'. But we are likely to come to a different conclusion.

On examining the text, we are immediately impressed by the tact and care with which it has been composed. Evidently Paul felt the delicate nature of his task. Yet there is nothing 'sticky' or awkward about it. In fact, having gently prepared the way, Paul is extraordinarily bold in his request. It is no grudging forgiveness that is asked for, but that Onesimus should be given a royal welcome, such as might be expected if the apostle were the one arriving!

It is not overfulsome to say that the whole letter breathes the atmosphere of Christian love. In the deepest sense it is a family letter about a family matter, from brother to brother concerning a

[5] Lohse, p. 188.

third brother. It is written to a man whose loving actions are widely known and valued (verses 4-7). Its appeal is *for love's sake*, though Paul might well have used his apostolic authority, and does indeed still expect obedience (verses 8-14, 21), and, most important, it is in essence a call to recognize Onesimus for what in truth he now is—*a beloved brother* (15-20).

It is in verse 16 that the heart of the letter is to be found. These marvellous words are worth studying with care, for they are a true charter of liberation. First, Onesimus is to be received back *no longer as a slave*. E. F. Scott has some words of caution here.[6] At the same time we can easily underestimate the force of this dramatic phrase. If Paul encouraged slaves to take their freedom when offered (though not to be over-anxious about it),[7] we may believe that he encouraged Christian masters, where possible, to grant it. How better could such a master express his conviction that his slave is now *more than a slave*, even *a beloved brother?* And this not only *in the Lord* (*i.e.* in the spiritual affairs of the congregation where we know that slaves had risen to positions of great responsibility), but also *in the flesh* (*i.e.* in the everyday affairs of work and business).

We are justified in concluding, therefore, that, if not by the letter of the law, yet in everything that made slavery a vile, degrading and loathsome practice, it must by such an appeal have been forthwith abolished within any Christian community.

It seems impossible to avoid this dramatic conclusion; and it is supported by the hints contained in verses 14 and 21. It has been suggested that Paul is really asking that Onesimus should be returned to Rome to continue his ministrations to him. But verse 22 *(I am hoping ... to be granted to you)* makes this unlikely. A much more attractive interpretation is to suppose that when Paul comes to Colossae he wishes Philemon to release Onesimus to be his fellow worker on future journeys, *i.e.* a new Timothy. In such a quite new situation the way would be open for Onesimus to

---

[6] 'It is not suggested that Onesimus, because he has now become a Christian, should be given his freedom. We miss the point of the letter altogether if we conceive of Paul as dealing with a serious offence in a purely sentimental fashion. He insists that the deserter should return to the post of duty and henceforth show himself faithful, and even face punishment if it should be dealt out to him. This was the only way in which he could prove that his conversion had been genuine.' Scott, *ad loc.*

[7] 1 Cor. 7:21-24

receive the just and loving treatment that would set him free to develop his full potential and capacities as a man and a Christian.

Meanwhile we can be sure that Philemon would now receive from this new man in Christ the true and willing service that is demanded of a servant of Christ (verse 11). It is necessary to see this side of the equation as well. It is not simply that Christianity has bestowed on a man a new freedom: it has also radically altered that man so that he is able to exercise it aright.

Once we grasp something of the miraculous transformation of human affairs brought about by the gospel in these young churches of the New Testament, we are better able to appreciate the patterns and priorities of apostolic involvement in society's problems. What was being achieved everywhere was the establishment of little oases where an alternative way of life was being practised and could be observed. This powerful leaven must do its work. Yet it is absurd to speak as though eighteen long centuries must elapse before the leaven did its predestined work through Wilberforce's triumph. In Paul's time a new day was already dawning for slaves in a multitude of households as the Word of God advanced in its triumphant progress.

Is it not also mistaken to speak as though the great, though scandalously delayed, achievements of emancipation in the nineteenth century settled the matter for good, and would never be betrayed, perhaps in other forms? We are wiser now than those 'apostles' of optimism whose attractive message filled the western world (at least) from the end of the last century until nearly our own day. As the light of Christ has receded, the darkness has encroached again, bringing with it other hideous tyrannies, even if at first their real nature has been hidden. When modern investigators can tell us that the life of the ordinary Chinese (one-fifth of the human race) is one of perpetual serfdom, and when in modern Soviet society men and women have lost all their real freedoms to a master State, and when extreme right-wing regimes oppress minorities and torture dissidents, it is not time to speak as though human enslavement were a thing of the past.

But if we protest against these things in the name of Christ, the question still remains why Paul did not do so. It does not seem quite satisfactory to give a pragmatic answer, however true, that such a crusade against slavery would have succeeded only in making the lot of slaves, especially those associated with the new faith, infinitely harsher rather than more hopeful. It is probably nearer the truth to say that such a campaign would have indelibly stamped the new movement as a dangerous and revolutionary political force, to be ruthlessly crushed. And this, to Paul, as to our Lord, would have been a betrayal of the character of the gospel.

For Paul, there is a clear line of demarcation between the world and the church: to him the world is essentially unchanged and unchanging, for in every generation the seeds of decay and disruption are born again. An anology may be of service here. The apostles never mount a campaign against that other enormous evil, war. For them it is axiomatic that the fact of war is a fact of life until the end of this age.[8] Nor does it appear that Christ and his apostles demand of believers non-involvement in the perils of their compatriots in times of national danger. In short, Christians must live and suffer in an evil world. At the same time, the new-born Christian is called to be a vigorous peacemaker, whether in family matters or in the larger affairs of people and nations, and the church is to be a community of peace in a world of war.

It also remains true that human tyranny will not cease until Christ returns. People will continue to oppress and exploit their fellows. Human bondage, in one form or another, will continue in a fallen world, bringing with it ever new examples of suffering, loss, indignity and shame. To live in this evil world Christians cannot avoid living within social structures that are unjust and unequal, though their presence within it as salt and light should help to change structures. Yet, whether one is born an 'Onesimus' or a 'Philemon', one can find in Christ the secret of spiritual freedom: in addition, 'Philemon' has the power, the opportunity and the responsibility to liberate the captive in more material and practical ways.

If this perspective is correct, the narrowness of Paul's aim becomes of fascinating significance. A burning appeal to an unknown house-church in Phrygia is his way to begin to change the world! It is decidedly less impressive than a grand pronouncement of an ideal to a wider audience. But long after such rhetoric would be forgotten (and its life is conspicuously short), the influence of a letter like this would spread from life to life and from group to group, in the Lycus valley, and wherever its inhabitants journeyed.

[8] Mk. 13:7–8.

Not that we are likely to learn these lessons from Paul until once again we are persuaded of the incorrigible sinfulness of mankind (dreams of a 'great society' so often remain dreams), and of the extraordinary power of the gospel in the local churches to bring back hope into a world increasingly without it.

Brief notes

a. The greeting (verses 1-3)

Paul's normal description of himself as an apostle would be inappropriate here. Yet it is suggestive that this emphasis on himself as *a prisoner* is so marked in one short letter (verses 9, 13, 23). Is it that Paul would remind us that freedom is not an absolute right or necessity, without which people cannot fulfil their proper destiny? At least his chains absolve the apostle from all unfeeling glibness when he calls upon Onesimus to give up his liberty and return home.

b. The thanksgiving (verses 4-7)

The difficulty of verse 6 is illustrated by some tortuous and laboured translations (*e.g.* RV). But we should not fail to notice the close links with Paul's patterns of thought in Colossians. There too, *love* is the hallmark of authentic Christian goodness; there love is always a fruit of faith; there love needs development through knowledge:[9] there, all that we need for full reconciliation with God is in Christ, and here, all that we need for full reconciliation with one another is likewise in Christ.

c. The appeal (verses 8-21)

Chiefly significant is Paul's identification of Onesimus with himself. Onesimus is his child (verse 10), has proved useful to him (verse 11), is his *very heart* (verse 12). He would gladly keep Onesimus with him (verse 13), for he is now such a beloved brother to him (verse 16). Onesimus is to be received as they would receive Paul (verse 17), and his debts charged to Paul's account (verse 18!), for it is by treating his returning slave generously that Philemon will refresh the heart of Paul (verse 20).

The force of all this could not be lost on Philemon. It would be

[9]Col. 1:8, 4, 9.

190

impossible now to treat as a lesser being one who enjoyed such close fellowship with the great apostle. And might he not hope that a man who had proved himself of such value to Paul would be just such a brother and helper to himself and all under his roof?